DISCOVER YOUR TRUE IDENTITY

The Lily
in the Valley

KEZIA DAVIS

Queen E Publication

The Lily in the Valley: Discover Your True Identity
Copyright © 2013 by Kezia Davis

Cover Designer: AMB Branding Design
Cover Designer Editor: Abadullah Safdar
Book Interior Designer: Deasy Suryani Purba
Editor: Anca Popescu
Distributed by: CreateSpace, a DBA of On-Demand Publishing, LLC

Library of Congress Control Number: 2013920763
ISBN-13: 978-0615919478
ISBN-10: 0615919472

Printed in the United States of America

10 9 8 7 6 5 4 3 2 1

This book is dedicated to my daughter
Allanah Davis and my two sisters
Audrianna & Faith Davis.

Also for the youth who battles with peer
pressure, acceptance and self image. For
the those who are struggling to find your
own self identification.

For you who are battling with unforgiveness,
fear, doubt, shame, emptiness, depression,
people-pleasing.

*"This one thing I do, forgetting those things which
are behind and reaching forth unto those things which
are before, I press on toward the mark for the prize of the
high calling of God in Christ Jesus."*

Philippians 1: 13-14

Thanks for Caring

First and foremost I would like to give honor and praises to God up above, just for being who He is. He has not given up on me and I thank Him for making it possible for me to share my thoughts and yet another book. To the most important person in my life, my reason for living, my angel, ALLANAH DAVIS.You're such a jewel and out of all the blessings that God has already given me, I thank Him so much more for you. I can't and I will not ever forget my darling grandmother, QUEEN ESTER DAVIS, you are my mother and now my guardian angel. Although you're not here with me in the present, you still illuminate me with your presence in my dreams and in my heart. I will never be able to describe how much I love you and I will never be able to express how thankful I am for you. God blessed me again, when He allowed someone like you to raise me. To yet another blessing from God, JAMES DAVIS, thanks so much for being the best father you can be to our daughter. I thank you for your help, your generosity, and your love. To my father GUYRE HARRIS, thanks so much for being there and for always giving me much needed advice. To my sisters FAITH & AUDRIANNA DAVIS, thank you so much for always being there when I need you. You two are irreplaceable, wouldn't choose any other sisters if someone paid me. To my sister, from another mother, VALENZIA BURKS, thanks so much for your support. Although you may be my cousin we are as close as sisters as anyone. I love you and I'm so thankful for you. You too are irreplaceable. To my birth mother, KAWANDA DAVIS, although I never got the chance to know you, I thank you, for giving me life. COURTNEY WILIAMS, what can I say...You have always been there to make me smile, to brighten my day, and to motivate me. Thanks so much for your loyalty, your love, your kindness, and your faith in me. You inspire me to be better. I have not forgotten about the rest of you who has played a major part in my life. To show my appreciation to those who have cared for me I've decided to say what I had to say to you all in a poem:

When someone is there to take the time to listen without judgment,
When someone reaches out and lend a helping hand,
When someone does something thoughtful without motive,
When someone makes you feel protected by always being there,
When someone senses there are times when you have special needs,
When someone gives you inner strength and courage to make it
by their words as well as their deeds,
When someone have the desire to take interest I just how you're
feeling, In those times those people need to know how appreciated and
special they are.
And from the bottom my heart I would like to say –
Thanks so much for caring!

THANKS FOR CARING:

My Brothers: Dalontay Davis, Tony Hill Jr. & Lionel Sears
My Adopted Mom: Brenda Davis
My Pa-Pa: Tony Hill Sr.
My Second Mother: Helen Beaty
My Best Friend: Latoya Porter
My Family: Dorothy Flowers, Sherry Davis, China Davis,
Catrina Davis, Grant Davis, Fred Davis, Aja Jones,
Patricia Stanley, Shamorra Walker, Sharkiran Major, Pam Davis,
Jessie Ransom, Michael Davis, Bernice Davis, Dexter Davis,
Treletha Davis, Gaye Nell Davis, Brenda Dumas, Santana Davis, Shadae
Dennard, Treletha Davis, Calvin Reese, Virginia Williams, Chequila Hayes,
Robert King, Rita King, Paula Golson
Sonny King, Jermaine Williams, Patriece Florence, Sharon Laster,
Gary Brown, Jr. Brown & to all my supporters.

Contents

Introduction

THE TITLE FOR this book serves a purpose. The Lily in the Valley represents facing situations (valleys) and overcoming those situations. All of us face valleys but after we learn the value that is in those valleys we are able to blossom like lilies. Let me help you understand the significance and meanings of valleys and lilies. Valleys are filled with purpose. They are eye-openers and teachers. In the valley is where we develop faith and strength. The funny part about a valley is one may fall into a valley but don't even realize it. In, a valley or *dale* is a *depression* with predominant extent in one direction. A very deep river valley may be called a *canyon* or gorge. Iyanla Vanzant gives a perfect example of what a valley is.

She defines it as a life situation designed to teach a character trait or spiritual virtue which has been undeveloped or under-developed during the course of your life. Traits and virtues that we know we should practice but forget or resist to incorporate in our lives, such as patience, faith, trust, courage, wisdom and honesty. A valley is that trial, that tribulation that you face. A valley is a dark experience that circulates around you, that addiction, that toxic waste you can't seem to get rid of, that job you're not satisfied with but need to have for the sake of your finances. A valley is feeling trapped in a situation with no way out. A valley is the unforgivness that is causing your body to slowly decay spiritually, physically, mentally and emotionally.

It's the battles you face with your body (diabetes, high blood pressure, cancer, AIDS, etc.) everyday without a cure. A valley is the peace, the love, the serenity and the tranquility that you lack but desire to have more of. A valley is staying in a relationship that you know you don't need but do it for the sake of "love" or loneliness. A valley is doing things that you know is no good for you   (drugs, alcohol, unprotected sex, prostitution, etc) but not having ability to or not wanting to find a way out. A valley could be having a lot of needs but not enough money to supply those needs. A valley is having enough money but not enough happiness. A valley can be all sorts of things and can come in all sorts of patterns and masquerades.

It takes work to get out of a valley. One must be able to do what it takes to get out of those valleys. Now the beautiful part about getting out a valley is that in each valley that we master we regain the petals to formulate our lily. God has planted a seed in all of us but it is up to us to take care of that seed so that our flower can blossom. Why a lily? Why not a rose or a sunflower? Many do not know this but a lily has a more attractive meaning to it. Lilies symbolize hope, faith, birth, purity, renewal, cleansing and transiting. After during further research I learned that with its three petals, the lily is often considered a "trinity symbol", holding the representation of three virtues: charity, hope and faith. Furthermore, parts of the lily have specific religious significance to the Virgin Mary:

- The stem of the lily symbolizes Mary's religiously faithful mind.
- Lily petals represent Mary's purity and virginity.
- The scent of the flower represents Mary's divinity.
- The leaves signify her humility.

I researched a little harder and discovered that *in symbolic dreams*, lily meaning deals with the sanctity of the heart, elegance and a need for clarity or cleansing. Dreaming of lilies could mean the time is right to act upon a long-thought upon plan. Further, it indicates that we are coming into a fuller integration of ourselves and developing personal balance. It is also a sign that we are seeking rest, peace and tranquility. In esoteric and mystery teachings, lily meanings includes: development, growth, progress and freedom. Today's youth are not being educated enough about life nor are they being encouraged enough. In this book I not only speak to adults I am also speaking to the young man who does not have a male role model and the young woman who was never told that beauty is really only skin deep. I hope that whoever read this book gets a full understanding of it and I pray that it helps you discover your true identity. When God changes us, everything around us changes. After you have been through the valley and have experience growth, freedom, peace, change, faith, love, etc., then you know that the lily implanted inside of you has bloomed; that same seed that God implanted inside of you. You have bloomed and became a new creature or should I say lily.

"Therefore if any man be in Christ, he is a new creature: old things are passed away: behold all things become new".
2 Corinthians 5:17

Loving Your Inner You
You are the Gift

"Knowing others is intelligence; knowing yourself is WISDOM.
Mastering others is STRENGTH; knowing yourself is POWER."
                                                      ~ Lao Tzu

Loving Your Inner You *You are the Gift*

1

MANY PEOPLE struggle with who they are,what they are, whose they are, and how to find fulfillment that is needed to enable them to discover what they do not know. Many people struggle in life because they feel as though they know who they are and what they need, when it fact, they only act on their fleshly desires (want). It will be hard for anyone to understand and grasp their true calling without consulting, discovering, and accepting their Creator. Love is a beautiful thing, but people have created their own perspectives and manifestations of love that causes people to behave in ways that does not initially demonstrate love. They want love and want to be loved, yet they know nothing about the art of loving. Pure, authentic and unadulterated love is not orchestrated by lust, control, and power (which is the attributes of Satan), but by a love that's agape and fulfilling, which comes from the Creator love... God. Love is understood yet, attaching selfish thoughts and motives is what causes the imbalance. People find themselves caught up in a toxic situation in which they define as love and totally lose themselves. Their selfishness overcrowds their judgment, causing them to lose focus on who they are and who they always wanted to be. Who they once were and who they have allowed someone to change them into becoming; blinds them from seeing their inner self and the gift.

A person will never know what the gift is until they take the wrappings from around the box and then open it up to see what's inside. In the same way, you will never see the gift inside of you unless you rip off the wrapping from around you. There's nothing more important than knowing who you are and loving who you are from the inside and out. Understand that before you were born, God already had a plan for you. He knew what you were going to look like, what you were going to be doing in your life and who you were going to be doing it with. He allows situations to play out in our lives in order for Him to come in and change the situation and get His glory. He likes to show off! He likes to blow your mind!

When He formulated you in His mind, He gently and creatively began to form you from your head down to your toes. He saw no flaws, nothing lacking and nothing missing. The texture of your hair is what He wanted it to be, the size of your head was shaped, the framing of your face to blend in with your eyes, nose, lips and ears. When He began to make your body, He already knew whether you'd be short, curvaceous, slim or tall. I do not believe that we are all meant to be skinny. Just because the society recommends it doesn't mean that it is what God intended for you to look like. We are all different; with different features and different body frames that makes us all unique.

It is important that we keep our bodies healthy but that doesn't mean that you should be skinny in order to be healthy. There are many skinny people out there that are unhealthy because of their lack of exercise and eating habits. The point of it all is that in everything God makes, He sees it as good. When He made the Earth, He looked and was very well pleased with the job He'd done. When He created you, He looked with love, compassion and joy. Just as He was pleased with the Earth, in the same way He was pleased with you. You weren't placed on this Earth for nothing, nor was it by mistake. We all serve a purpose on this Earth, whether it's to change the world or to help someone in this world. You have to believe that you are good, you are valuable, and you are needed. You play a major role in the plans of God and you FIT! He'd created in all of us a gift that one couldn't take away from the other. He created you. You are the gift!

After my grandmother died I had become real careless and rebellious over time. For a while I was very angry, not sure who I was really angry at. I had my own insecurities and I did not realize the gift or the plan that God had for my life. I made a bunch of careless decisions and I jumped from relationship to relationship trying to find completeness or someone to show me love and in every relationship that I had I could find no satisfaction. That empty spot in my heart was never filled. I tried to find love in the wrong places and faces only to end up feeling more worthless then I did before. Then there was one guy I dated, who I will call for the sake of a lawsuit, John that said something to me that stuck with me.

He said, "Don't you know your worth? Don't you know that you are worth more than gold?" I was going through a bad situation with a guy, who I will call Jim that had broken my heart. There I was crying in John's arms about Jim. He had no idea what I was going through and he later told me that it didn't matter what I was going through but he'd known I was hurting. He loved me like I loved Jim, but I figured I felt the same about him as Jim felt about me. It's funny how you can treat the person who loves you the most just like the person who loves you the least treats you. Anyway, what he said to me opened my eyes and rattled my mind; a man had never told me that.

He'd spoken life into me even when I felt like I had died when my grandmother did. My body was here on earth but my soul was in the grave with her. I didn't feel worthy. I didn't feel like I was needed. Even after I had my daughter, the empty void could not be filled. I was still going through my valley of self-worth. All my broken pieces were all over the place. I didn't know she would be the one to help me mend those broken pieces back together again. I had not yet figured out that she was my gift given to me nor had I figured out that I was indeed a gift from God with a gift that He'd installed in me while creating me. Although I'd known God, I was faced with situations in my life at the time that He seemed foreign to me. How can you begin to love your inner you and realize you are the gift:

DISCOVER YOUR PURPOSE

Identify with the fact that you were born for a purpose, with a purpose, and on purpose. Ask God to help you discover your purpose. It could already be in front of you. Think of something that you are most good at that can help change some aspect of the world. God gives each of us gifts. In 1 Corinthians 12: 4-11 it says, "There are different kinds of gifts, but the same Lord. There are different kinds of service, but the same Lord. There are different kinds of working, but the same God works all of them in all men. Now to each one the manifestation of the Spirit is given for the common good. To one there is given through the Spirit the message of wisdom, to another the message of knowledge. To another faith to another gifts of healing by that one Spirit. To another miraculous powers, to another prophecy, to another distinguishing between spirits, to another speaking in different tongues, and to still another interpretation of tongues. All of these are the work of one and the same Spirit, and He gives them to each one, just as He determines."

Let's jump to Ephesians 4: 11 further explaining saying, "It is He who gave some to be apostles, some to be prophets, some to be evangelists, and some to be passion and teachers, to prepare God's people for works of service, so that the body of Christ may be built up." We are all placed on earth to service one another and through that service God get's all the glory. Now don't mix your purpose and/or gift up with your own dreams and desires. Just like Steve Harvey said, "Why try to be a singer, knowing you can't sing." Just because you see Beyonce', Whitney Houston, Jennifer Hudson, Mariah Carey, Deitrick Haddon, Taylor Swift, Yolanda Adams or Jay Z parading around on the stage in the spotlight, you want the same, but lack the gift. If you know you scared of blood then why would you want to be a surgeon or phlebotomist?

I hear many people in the church ordain people to preach, but not every one is meant to become a preacher. Many are called, but few are chosen. It is true...that we can do all things in Christ who strengthens us. But who said God strengthen you to do that? It's not what people call you, but it's what you answer to from God. God has placed a gift in each and every one of us, so embrace the gift that He has given you. He gave you the gift for a reason. If you know that what you're doing is not what God placed in you to do, then allow God to re-direct you, so you can start walking into your purpose. If you know God given you a vision, then you must make the effort to bring that vision in fruitation. Be obedient, follow God's prompting. Trust in the Lord with all your heart and lean not on your own understandings, in all your ways acknowledge Him and He will direct your paths (Proverbs 3:3-6).

Only God knows who we are and what we were place on earth to do. You can't and will not ever be able to discover your life's meaning by looking within yourself or determining in your own mind as to what you *think* you should be doing. I'm sure you've tried that already. You didn't create yourself, so how can you tell yourself what you were created for or what your purpose is? Start with God; after all He is the only one who can give you the answer. Ask Him what in the world was you put on earth to do. Ask Him, how you can be of service to Him. Understand that you only exist because it was His will for you to. You were made by God and for God, not the other way around—and until you realize that, life will never make sense to you.

It's only in God that you will discover your true origin, identity, significance, meaning, purpose and your destiny. With God on your side, walk towards your purpose and know that He will never lead you astray and when you're tired of walking and feel like giving up He will carry you. He will create in you another being and restore and rebuild you. Now let's go back to the part when I said people want the gifts that God has not prepared them for or has not given them. Seek ye' FIRST, the kingdom of God. Don't just formulate in your mind that you are destined to do something just because you like doing it. I'm not telling you not to enjoy your hobbies or not to sing, but what I am telling you is that if you do not know your purpose or have not walked into the purpose that God has for you, then you're not living your life in the fullness of God. It's like walking in the wilderness, trolling back and forth with no direction. I too had to seek God for my purpose and for a vision. Until this day, I constantly talk to God and try not to react or make decisions without His approval. God wants us to be purposeful and live in our purpose but how can we do that if we are so busy seeking out our own understanding and not His?

Now before I begin making this statement I just want to clear the air before you go assuming and getting all mad at what I am about to say. Now I know God loves it and recommend that we seek His face and ask Him for stuff, but some of us take it to the extreme. God has no problem with us coming to Him for things, as a matter of fact, He recommends that we do, but there is some stuff people ask God for or ask Him to take out of their lives that they aren't even prepared or ready for. You want God to send you a husband or wife but you are not even husband or wifey material. We want Him to constantly bring or give us something that we aren't even prepared for.

You want Him to give you a good job but you fail to obtain the experience needed to get the job. You ask God for money but you don't even wisely spend the little money that is already given to you. How are you going to ask God to show you who is not for you or to take someone out of your life if you can't even let go? The word says that you reap what you sow. You have to make the effort and take a step in digging up the dirt to plant your seed. What you sow is most of time what you reap whether good or bad. Not only do you have to dig up the dirt but you have to put the seeds in the ground, cover the seeds, put your fertilizer on it and then allow God to shine His sun on it, water it with His rain and then you can watch it grow.

Work with Him and He'll work with you. Yes, the Lord takes pleasure in those who seek Him with a humbled and sincere heart. He delights in those who seek Him for help. He loves it when we have faith enough to depend on Him for direction. But still, God not only have a desire to want you, but He wants you to be accessible to Him. Change the way you come at God. Surprise yourself and ask Him what you can do for Him rather than what He can do for you. Often times we take advantage of God because we know what He can do. We must self-reflect and think about how we can be of service to Him. We must learn to be obedient to God and not always come to Him in our time of selfish and insincere desperation. Many people have the tendency to use God for their own self-actualization.

They want God to move when they say move or answer when they want Him to. They want Him to be their own personal servant that serves to their self-centered and selfish desires. I cannot stress this enough, GOD IS THE CREATOR, NOT YOU! YOU WERE MADE FOR GOD, NOT THE OTHER WAY AROUND! Life is about letting God use you for His purposes, not you using Him for your own purpose. Often time we take advantage of God because we know what He can do. We must self-reflect and think about how we can be of service to Him. We must learn to be obedient to God and not always come to Him in our time of selfish and in sincere desperation. If God treated us like we treated Him we'll all be messed up. When things aren't going so well we call on the name of Jesus. It is then that we discover who He is and what He's able to do. T.D. Jakes and I have an understanding. He speaks words of wisdom that agrees with my spirit. We come into agreement when it comes to knowing who God is we both understand that He was God, before we even realized it. He was justified before hand, so He doesn't need us to justify who He is. Please, understand that God already knew who He was before anybody was there to tell Him who He was. He already knew that He was able.

He already knew that He was a healer before He healed you. He already knew He was a provider before He provided for you. He already knew He was God all by Himself. God doesn't need to be reassured but it is necessary that we glorify Him and praise Him for what He has already done and what He plans to do. Not just during the bad times but in the good times too. How in the world would we be able to wake up each morning? How many times have you waken up without acknowledging what God really can do and without giving Him thanks for life, good health and strength? I am saying we because even I have been guilty of using God when I saw fit.

Calling Him when I was in trouble or needed Him to get me out of some mess I'd created just to go back into my mess when He brought me out. When the last time you'd taken a look around and saw all the beauties God have gifted us with? Look at the sky, the stars in the moon, the oceans, lakes and ponds, the tress, the flowers, the birds, the bees, and the leaves. Look around you, God has always been good. He has always been amazing, creating wonders that mankind would never be able to figure out. He's always proven what He is capable of doing. People only see the power of God when He reveals Himself to them. Was it when He spared your life that you realized how good He is? Was it when you knew you could have been in prison for life, but instead, you got off. Or was it when He protected your body from AIDs, HIV, and other sexual transmitted disease, after you offered your temple to many who was not deserving...Did you realize how good your God is when the doctor said you will not live for a certain amount of time because of your illness (cancer, heart failure, etc), but God said you will not die but you will live? God did not create us to use Him but to acknowledge that we need Him in our daily lives. When you discover your purpose, with God's help, then you will be able to get a vision of what can be and find out who you really are.

ANALYZE YOURSELF. WHO ARE YOU?

Analyze yourself without deduction or addition. Who are you? Do you know everything there is to know about yourself? I mean who are you *really?* Not the person you become around your friends or mate; not the person you become in a professional setting; not the person you have tricked yourself into becoming; not the person someone has told you, you are or should be; not the person you have consistently tried to be to please yourself and others. Whose the *real* you? Open yourself up and get to know you for yourself, then ask God to show you your flaws and the things that you need to change in you. Allow Him to reveal everything to you, that way you'll know everything there is to know about you.

Now that can be scary, yet refreshing to the point that you no longer hold yourself in contempt. Being real with you can be painful because you have denied yourself and looked over who you are for so long that you believe the lies that you told or someone has told to you. Another thing, stop listening to folks who tell you that you will never be anything or won't amount to anything. They are only revealing how they feel about themselves and want you to be the way that they are. If you knew who you really were, then nobody would be able to speak stupidity into your life. When I really got my life together and decided to give all of me to God, was when I really sat down and dissected myself. There is nothing like being real with yourself and accepting the things you didn't know about you; the good, bad and the ugly parts.

I'd learned how to accept who I am, know who I was and love myself despite of what was told to me or the mistakes I'd made along my path in life. There is this brilliant and anointed author and motivational speaker name Iyanla Vanzant, if you ever read any of her books or listened to any of her speeches you will agree with me. When I read her books, they help me in a way that I didn't think possible. I often say God had to be speaking through Iyanla in those books specifically for me. Everything that I had digested from her readings made so much sense to me. I felt her words in my mind and heart and her books made me motivational towards achievement in life and made me believe and love God even the more. She helped me understand "The Law of Self-Knowledge." The Law of Self-Knowledge (To Thine Oneself Be True) is to be totally truthful to yourself.

There was a passage in her book that really stuck to me and I felt would be very motivational for my readers to know as well. You got to know who you are if you want to make sense of everything around you otherwise you will only dictate your life on what others want you to be, how you think you should behave and what they think you should become. So with the help my darling motivator Iyanla Vanzant from her book titled "The Value in the Valley", we both agree that the best thing to do to be able to be true to you is to: Listen to your heart. Follow to its prompting. Honor what you feel accordingly. When we break this law we become pawns in the game of life. People can convince us that we are what we are not, and lead us to believe that we are not what we are. Be able to identify your original thoughts from those you have adopted. It also means, trust that you can have an original thought and act upon it even when others are not "pleased" by what you are doing. Self- acceptance means embracing all of you.

"You cannot heal what you will not face." *~James Baldwin*

Be the best you that you can be! Stop denying who you are and what you feel. Stop criticizing yourself. Take a look in the mirror at least three times a day and tell yourself "I LOVE YOU', "I AM JUST RIGHT", "I AM PURPOSEFUL", "ONLY I CAN BE WHO I BELIEVE I AM". Young lady, look at yourself and believe in you. You don't need someone else to tell you your worth, you are already worthy. You don't need a boy to tell you you're beautiful, the beauty is already in you. Stand for what you know, no matter what nobody tells you. If they don't like what you're saying then dismiss them they weren't meant to be in your life anyway. If you are around someone who is always into something and pursues you to do something when you know it isn't right then you need to change your friends. Pretty soon you'll realize Jesus and you are your only true friends. Young man, you don't have to wear your pants off your butt and talk slang to be a part of something.

If your "boys" can't accept who you are then you will have to let them go and find some new "boys". Find some friends who want an education and a better future. Have some friends that respect your wishes and who do not condone wrong doing. Can't nobody make you into something you're not unless you take the lead to do something that is not like you. When we know who we are, we become aware of how we function. When we are aware of how we function, we are not as ready and willing to accept what people say about us. The true value of awareness is that it provides us with the courage and strength to resist those people and conditions that do not reflect the true image of who we are. Be real with you! Respect the truth! And find ways to better you! In my valley of self-awareness and self-evaluation, I came to the conclusion that I definitely didn't know who I was or what I wanted to do with my life.

In those valleys I couldn't believe the results that came up. I couldn't believe that most of the problems that I had was with me. I had no idea that I did not fully like myself. I couldn't believe that the people who I allowed in my life was a representation of me and how I felt about myself. Can you believe my attitude and how I treated others resulted into the outcome of my life? Can you believe I was very demanding in my relationships in both dating and with God? You mean to tell me that I'd put God in a little box and all this time been driving myself without becoming the passenger? I can't believe that I was hard on others as well as myself because I didn't understand the true value of love. Can you believe I had an attitude problem and that I was really bitter and mean? Wow, it's unbelievable for me to think that I was abuser.

I abused my body with marijuana and alcohol (was never really a big drinker though) because I told myself that it will help get rid of the pain from my existing problems. I abused the men that I was dating either physically and/or emotionally when I couldn't get my way or when I wanted things my way because if I wasn't in charge it made me feel weak and not in charge of my life. It means that if I allowed someone to get close to my heart they would eventually break it. I had a guard over my heart and it eventually had become ice solid, holding no hostages. I said I would never be like the people who helped "raised" me. Now it was like a punch in the gut when I realized that I had some of if not all of their ways. I didn't realize that my child sees all my actions and it could have an affect on her. No way, nobody could tell me that I was a bad parent. I'd always taken care of my child and never asked anybody for anything in return.

Then the truth hit me again, I was impatient, distant and a little too mean to my child. I didn't play with her enough, read books to her when she wanted me to before she went to bed. I'd put fear in her because of my short temper and many times I'd scream at her for little reasons. She'd become scared to talk to me, scared to ask me anything and afraid of me completely. Yes, I provided her with clothes, food and shelter but I didn't provide her with the time or unconditional love that goes beyond material and worldly things. I'd failed. I'd failed too show my child the unconditional love that I promised I would show her considering that I didn't get if from my parents growing up. I promised that I would never abandon her but instead I will always be there if she needed someone to talk to.

If I had to climb the highest mountains and swim the deepest sea just to get to her aid, I promised my child that I would. I was too impatient or "spending time with myself" to help her with her homework, go to most of her school functions and praise her when she's doing a good job. Yes, I did go to her parent-teacher conference meetings and even went to her class a few times to help out as well as joined the school board as the chair of the yearbook committee. However, I started going to interact with her at school less and less to the point where I failed to go at all. Of course I allowed her to be in extracurricular activities that I wasn't in growing up, she did gymnastics and karate but I didn't won't to play any games with her and anything else that took me from what I was doing. I got so lazy or busy doing my own thing, that

I didn't no longer have time to watch her in her karate classes then I took her out of them because I didn't *feel* like taking her.

I realized that I was present but not fully active in her life. Could it have been because my paternal mother wasn't there for me to do all those things for me? I mean is there anyone to blame for my distance and resistance to be what I needed and wanted to be as a parent? After all the things I've done I still wasn't satisfied with myself. There was still something about me that I didn't like. I wanted more in my life, period. I was still working towards ways to satisfy my own feelings of need, lack of self-worth and lack of fulfillment. I wanted the perfect man, that I could put a check mark on every point on my list of the perfect man. You know the list; whether you admit it or not we all have one. We all think about the man or woman we would love to marry. Here I am and there I was a published author, a fairly good radio host and a college graduate but I still felt I had not done enough.

There it was...the truth that blew me away... How can I want more but do not seek more? How could I ask for more, when I was constantly accepting less? How can I be purposeful if I didn't believe that I was purposed and/or that I was worthy enough to do that in which I was purposed for? Do you mean to tell me that I'd given up on myself because of one mistake I made years ago? How can I give advice to someone about the same things I'm struggling with? How can I tell someone to forgive but has yet to forgive? I couldn't tell someone to seek God, do "exactly" what He tells you to do, when He tells you to do it, when I was not even doing it myself. How can I tell someone to fervently pray, read the Word daily, and constantly meditate on the God, when I was failing in these areas. My lack of faith in God was apparent and the facts were there. Do you mean to tell me that the measure of faith God planted inside me was nonexistent to me? That all I'd studied about God and all He's brought me through, that I'd still had doubt in His abilities?

That I still couldn't trust Him unless He'd give me some miraculous sign showing me that it was indeed Him? My faith was weaker than my praise. My belief was weaker than my prayers. I'd allowed the devil to have too much access to my mind that he knew all the right buttons to push, when to strike when I was weak and what to say when my flesh got in the way of my total belief in God. I'd been too much for too long by myself and for my own satisfaction. I needed to get myself together and stop playing. When I finally decided to allow God to take over and accept who I was and what I had become I begin to ask God for change, to upgrade and extract some things in and out of me. I asked Him to renew my mind, give me the understanding of true love, to give me wisdom and knowledge. To open my eyes to the things I could not see and to change my attitude as well as my mindset.

I also asked Him to get rid of unhealthy association. If they are in my life without purpose then I didn't need them in my circle. I want friends that love God and do the will of God. I have always been choosy as to who I associate with but this time instead of me choosing, God will be the one that does it. In order to change who you are, you must change what you've become. Change your mindset. I've given advice to many people who wanted me to answer their questions but refuse to take the advice and apply it. You don't know how many times I've had to repeat the same things to some people. I got to the point where I had to tell them, "Look if you're not ready to take the steps to do what it takes to change the situation then don't ask me anything." I had come to realize that if people continue to stay stuck in their situation then they either like the feeling of or is not fully ready to get up out of it. Some people like pain, the only way that they can function properly is through pain. If you are one of the ones that feel you have been struggling all your life then it's you who have a problem.

Nobody should have to struggle all their lives. You have to have the mind and the willingness to change and to overcome struggles. You struggle because you stay stuck in that struggle. You have to change what you're doing in order to make a change. I was listening to a sermon from T.D. Jakes one day and he said some things that really took to me, he said, "you have to fix the mind before you can bestow the blessings because until they get their mind right everything you invest in them is going to leak out of the crevasses of a mind that refuses to change." You have to have the mind to change. You have to get rid of every poison and inflexibility that is keeping you from changing for the better. Ask for a new mind! Lord give me a new mind! As I said before, we think we know who we are when we have no idea. It is the saying that, "can't nobody know me more than I know me." I beg to differ.

Since we are capable of lying to ourselves we fail to be able to know who we really are. Our actions speak for itself. The way we treat people speaks for itself. What we do to ourselves and how we present ourselves speak for itself. People are able to see the things we fail to see or do not won't to see. Have you ever noticed how you can be around a person for so long that they know what you're thinking, what you were going to say or do when you do it and say it, how you scramble your eggs, what your reaction would be to a certain situation and so on and so forth? How someone has the capability of speaking on your behaviors, feelings and emotions without understanding why? That's because they have been able to see who you really are based on your actions, your body language and how you present yourself to be. A person only knows what you reveal to them. If it looks like a duck and quack like a duck, then guess what? AFLACK.

DISCOVER WHAT LOVE FEELS LIKE

To discover what love feels like is to first seek its Creator. For God is love. In order to get the full advantage of love, you have to be open to receiving love by receiving God. Then as you receive love you'll get an understanding of how it feels and He will teach you how to love yourself and others as He shower His love upon you. It is important that you love yourself. If you do not love yourself then you cannot and you will not be able to love another. If you don't love yourself enough to live in your own integrity nor have a solid sense of self-value and self-worth, then loving other people will in fact be very difficult for you. After feeling His love, then you will be able to come to the realization that the love you thought you knew was nothing compared to the love He'd filled in you. God's love is the type of love that you will never get from man. This type of love is unordinary; you can't get it from just anybody. You can't buy it. There's no drug out there that's more addictive.

Sex can't fill it. Nobody else obtains it. You can search all over and you will never be able to compare it. When you get His love you want feel the need to have a man/woman around to just have someone to hold and say they love you. You'll no longer put up with Tom and worry yourself sick about where he's at. Or constantly blame yourself for what he is doing and trying to find ways to make him love you and forget about Judy. You won't have to keep trying to find ways to change Halley so she can be a suitable wife for you. She's not ready to marry you. She doesn't see anything wrong with going out to different clubs all the time and coming home when she get ready. When you're able to love yourself then your love will be stronger than any love Tom, Judy or Halley can give you. God's love can't be separated for I am a firm believer and I am witness to this fact. Even Paul the Apostle can vouch for this in saying, "For I am convinced that neither death nor life, neither angels nor demons, neither the present nor the future, nor any powers, neither height nor depth, nor anything else in all creation, will be able to separate us from the love of God that is in Christ Jesus our Lord (Romans 8:38-39)."

Let's go back to the story about Jim, now you already know how much I loved him. I was in love with him for about six years. All I thought about was him. I was so convinced that we would be together that I tried for years to convince him that I was the one for him. I was trying to help him believe in what I believed. I remember I'd made it my business to move back to my hometown from New York once he told me that he would be coming home from the service. He said he had something very important to tell me and my mind wondered and I made myself believe that he was going to ask me to marry him. What a thought... Well, let's just say when we finally talked marriage was far from his mind. He'd told me that he'd got this woman pregnant and that I shouldn't be mad because I got pregnant while "I was loving him". I tried to play it off and told him that it was all okay. Months later I moved to Florida with my best friend at the time and I had called him to see where our relationship was going. Silly me I still expected him to love me and want me. Well, my bubble was burst and my heart broke into pieces when I struggled to digest the words that were coming out of his mouth over the phone.

He'd told me that he didn't want to hurt me anymore and that he wasn't ready for what I was ready for. I'd never felt so low in my life. I felt like a fool and indeed I was a fool for love; foolishly in love for love. I was broken... It was like he'd taken my heart in his hands in squeezed all the blood from it. It was like he didn't hear a word that came out of my mouth. He didn't acknowledge what I'd done for him over the years and how much time I put into him. Whatever he asked of me I had done. I didn't know what to do and I felt like I was about to have a nervous break down. In that moment, my friend wasn't around and I was in her mother's apartment all by myself. There was nobody I could turn to or share my pain with. At that moment reality set in, everything that I'd known about God and from the Word began to sank in. I went back to my first love.

Without hesitation, I got on my knees and cried out to God; asking Him to forgive me for putting man over Him and over myself, to forgive me for putting so much love into a man that I couldn't even give to myself and that I didn't even give to Him. I asked Him to hold me, to comfort me through the pain.

Then I felt a warm feeling all over me that couldn't be compared. I felt light, I felt comforted, loved, reassured and held. That was the first time I felt God and knew that He would always be there. Out of everything I did, He answered, He heard my cry and He didn't ignore or dismiss me, but He filled me with a love that could never be replaced. The type of love that He fills you up with is pure, without motive and with sincerity. It's the type of love you can't explain if someone was to ask you. It's like a bundle of sweetness, of butterflies, of tingles and of warmth all coming to you at once. You wouldn't know what to do with it but just to embrace it and welcome it. There's no competition, leaving you with wanting more and more of it. It's like those cheddar flavored Pringles, "I bet you can't eat just one". When He puts His hands on you and hold you, it's nothing compared to your lover, your paternal parents or your friends.

When He puts His love inside of you, only then you will discover the true meaning of love and how it feels. Now you're able to apply that love into your life and into yourself. When you begin to love who you are from the inside and discover that underneath those wrappings that the gift inside is you. Take that gift, cherish it and store it in a safe place where nobody could steal it, break it, damage it or destroy it. When you're content with who you are then everything begins to fall in place and what you accepted before will no longer be tolerated. The stuff that you didn't understand will become clear to you. You will no longer allow just anyone to gain access to your internal house: your spirit, your emotions, your life, and your decision making. They will no longer have permission to break you down, speak negativity in your life, and discourage you; because now you are stronger, wiser and most of all you know that if God can love you enough to create you then there must be something about you that is worth all of it and above. You are a gift that can't be bought into stores. You can't be copied or duplicated. Look into a mirror and love the reflection that you see. Be of comfort to yourself, motivate yourself. You are priceless and you are a gift that is worth having. You are you and that alone makes you special.

The Power of Forgiveness

"To forgive is to set a prisoner free and to discover that all along the prisoner was you."~B. Smedes

The Power of Forgiveness 2

*H*AVE YOU EVER sat back and questioned yourself? Ever wondered where you could have been, what you could have done and what difference you could have made? Now, ask yourself why your goals couldn't be reached, why your dreams dwindled away as years past on. Will you point the fingers at someone else? Or will it be because of what happened to you in your past? Let it all go! Let the past be the past! Some say it's easier said then done, but only if the person makes it hard. I have come to realize that the majority of the people who tell me that they cannot forgive a person who did them wrong are handicapped by a mistaken understanding of what forgiving really is. Understand that the only person that can keep you from moving forward is YOU. People do not understand how much power a person can have over them if they don't forgive them. If a person can change your personality, emotions and attitude then they have power over you because they have the ability to change you from who you are to someone else.

My relationship with Jim didn't end after he told me about him getting another girl pregnant. Yes I'd ask God for His help and He did. Yes, I'd felt His touch and was lifted up, but my feelings for Jim didn't go away as fast as I thought they would. My heart was still in it and my feelings for him were unshakable. I still loved him, even when he told me that he didn't love me the same way. I still felt as though he owed me his love after all the time and effort I put into our relationship. I still thought he owed me some sort of closure and an explanation as to why I wasn't good enough. I wanted him to feel bad for hurting me, so I constantly brought up how his words and actions affected me. Even though I told him that I forgave him and could be his friend inside I hated him while still loving him. Crazy huh. That's what our kind of love does. Create crazy, toxic, and empty feelings that we mistake for love. The truth is we have the elements to love, but we don't understand the full concept of loving. I'd hated what he did to me. I hated that he could just move on while I was still in the same spot. I thought he'd taken advantage of my love and had his way with me whenever he wanted to just because he knew how deep my love was.

He could have said jump and I would have said how high. When he called I answered, when his brother died I was there to comfort him and when he needed some advice I'd freely given it to him. Although we both had broken up some time before, there was never a man that I will allow to get close to me. He was always, in my mind, my number one. Although we'd started dating other people I found myself trying to make him jealous and when that didn't work I thought by giving my virginity to another would make him recognize me. I made slick little comments just to get a reaction, he didn't feed into it. I tried to understand what it was that he didn't get. Maybe it was me who failed to see, failed to listen, failed to understand. Failed to GET IT!

For years I held a lot of things against him. How dare he move on towards the future when I was still stuck in our past? How could he not realize how bad he hurt me? Why couldn't he see the love in my eyes when he looked into mine? Why didn't he take notice to my behavior and my actions of love towards him? How in heaven's name did he not see the pain in my eyes when he broke my heart? Did he not see the tears that flowed from my eyes as he ripped my heart out of my chest? Did he not realize the effect that he had on me? For years I failed to do my part in relationships to make it work because of the pain I was holding on to. I simply couldn't forgive him but most of all I simply couldn't forgive me. The only way you can regain that power is through forgiveness. Jesus came on Earth, not only to show people who He is but God knew man needed to be forgiven so He sent His Son, Jesus, to deliver all mankind from the eternal consequences of their sins (1 John 4: 9-10).

In Isaiah 43:25, the Lord says to Jacob, "I, even I, am he who blots out your transgressions, for my own sake, and remembers your sins no more." How easy it is for God to forgive us and not bring it up again? If God can forgive us for our sins, then why can't we forgive another? When you do someone wrong, do you not seek and hope to be forgiven? "Do unto others as you will have them do unto you." Forgive like you would want someone to forgive you. Colossians 3:13 says, "Bear with each other and forgive whatever grievances you may have against one another. Forgive as the Lord forgave you." God has forgiven us numerous of times for our sins and the things we have done, even when we didn't deserve it. I know what they did to you hurt you. When you thought you can trust them they failed you. When you'd given all of you to them, they broke you down, but in order to win a fight is to forgive.

God has the power to forgive and has granted us with the ability to forgive others, just as we have been forgiven. "And when you stand praying, if you hold anything against anyone, forgive him, so that your Father in heaven may forgive you your sins" (Mark 11:25). "Do not judge and you will not be judged. Do not condemn, and you will not be condemned. Forgive, and you will be forgiven (Luke 6:37)." My mom, not paternally but legally, was not a person I could get along with. I'm going to be honest and admit that living with her was some of the worst days of my life. It was like living with Jekyll and Hyde. I never knew when she'll get mad at her husband and kick both of us out or when she would say something crazy to hurt my feelings. To avoid the blows that she would try to throw at my self-esteem and ego, I would smoke marijuana to numb myself. So that her negative words wouldn't matter.

At one point she called me a lesbian and also accused me of sleeping with her husband. Everyday wasn't the same and I can admit I've said and done some hurtful things over the years to her as well, but it started when I got fed up. When it seemed like we were on the right path and I was on the verge of trying to make our relationship work she will say or do something to mess it all up. At the time I couldn't understand that she had a problem with love herself. She was dealing with her own valleys. She too battled with love. She simply had no idea what love was. She'd had one husband that beat her and one husband that constantly cheated. Her own kids were wounded because of her lack of care for them, so why should I have expected more? She watched her father beat on her mother and she'd also suffered at the hands of her father as well. As I began to grow older I begin to fully understand her. She meant well but her lack of love and affection wasn't present because she didn't know what love does. She had a caring and beautiful mother but even her mother was dealing with her own problems.

She tried her best to love but how can a person love when their own self-esteem is crushed and the lack of love for themselves is unknown? To make a long story short, I forgave my mother long time ago but I'd gotten a little deeper at showing her when I was visiting Jacksonville, Florida. My Godfather had passed away and we were both staying at his daughter's house. She suggested that we pray and the power of God moved in that place. I went from silently praying to myself to interceding. God moved so heavily in me that even I wasn't prepared for it. I am happy that my mother and I prayed that night. Even though I had not talked to her in years, I yearned to have a relationship with her again. I wanted my mother around and in my life but I was just afraid that she'll hurt me again. I could see a change in her and although she is not perfect, that's okay because neither am I. I had come to realize that she has her own personal demons, past pains, and insecurities that she has to face and overcome.

We all make mistakes and we all fall short, but God has installed love in me that I am willing to spread to her. I am thankful that my mother is back in my life. I am grateful that God heard the yearnings in my heart. We are told in the Bible to love our neighbors as we love ourselves. The most remarkable and truthful thing about it is that we really do love our neighbors just as we love ourselves: we do unto others as we do unto ourselves. We are tolerant towards others when we tolerate ourselves. We forgive others when we have forgiven ourselves. We are prone to sacrificing others when we are ready to sacrifice ourselves. So it would be better to say, "Love our neighbors like Christ loved us" instead. Forgiveness is something that you have to sincerely have for another. God has given us the power to forgive! He wants us to receive the benefits of forgiveness. A spirit of unforgiveness complicates and compromises our daily walk with God. Forgiving others releases us from anger and allows us to receive the healing we need. Here is a prayer that uplifted me when I read it:

Father God, I need your help and your insights. Today I have gained a better understanding of forgiving others and with your help; I fully forgive from my heart. Just as you have freely forgiven me, I forgive them. Father, I ask you to forgive me for hurting others out of my own hurt and to heal my relationships with others. I pray all of this in Jesus' precious name and by whom all forgiveness and healing was made possible. Thank you for loving me in ways I'll never comprehend. In Jesus name, Amen.

You will know if you have forgiven a person because you won't keep bringing what they did to you back up. It will be lone forgotten and you will be at a level so high that it won't even have the same affect on you that it did before when you tell it to others or if it is brought up again. I do not believe that we can really forgive and forget nor do I believe it is healthy to do so. Forgetting that is. In my opinion, it is quite natural for us to remember and is important for us to do so for the sake of healing. Trying to pretend something didn't happen or that it really doesn't matter, when it really do, doesn't help us but keep us from denying how we truly feel. By remembering, we are able to face our problems and can eventually make the decision as to whether we want to forgive or not.

"Forgiving does not erase the bitter past. A healed memory is not a deleted memory. Instead, forgiving what we cannot forget creates a new way to remember. We change the memory of our past into a hope for our future." ~Beverly Flanigan

Beverly Flanigan made perfect sense to me in her book "Forgiving the Unforgivable: Overcoming the Legacy of Intimate Wounds" when she stated that, "Forgiveness has nothing to do with forgetting...A wounded person cannot--indeed, should not--think that a faded memory can provide an expiation of the past. To forgive, one must remember the past, put it into perspective, and move beyond it. Without remembrance, no wound can be transcended." Rev. Douglas Showalter further explains it by stating, "If we try not to remember, then we only bury the effect of the injury on us, such that we cannot truly resolve it and forgive the one who did it. In that way, the injury is not healed. Rather, it is like an infected wound which is closed prematurely. I also believe it is important to remember, so we can learn from our injuries, and try to protect ourselves and others from being injured in the same way again".

It took me years to realize how much stuff and unforgiveness I had pint up inside of me. The stuff that I didn't won't to admit or tried to bury. As I said in the previous chapter when my grandmother passed away I was very angry but wasn't sure who I was angry at. It took me a while to see that I was angry with God, myself and my grandmother. I was angry with God because He already knew that my grandmother was my caregiver, someone who I'd work so hard to please and the only person that was truly there for me and my two sisters. He had to know that we weren't going to be treated the same way she treated us. He had to know that we would be homeless, living from place to place and house to house. He had to know that we will have to fend for ourselves and settle for people who only put up with us because "we were their sister's daughters". He had to know that He was not only taking my grandmother but He was taking my mother AGAIN.

I'd already lost my paternal mother because a man didn't know how to keep his hands to himself or his genitals in his pants. My mother was a drug addict and shortly after she'd had my younger sister she went out and obviously thought she could trust the man who she grew up with, but he took advantage of her trust and raped, sodomized and strangled her with her bra (so I was told). God didn't you know the pain, the embarrassment and the shame that her kids would feel when they grew up to find out the details of their mother's murder. For a while I was ashamed to call my mother my mother. I was embarrassed to know that she was a crack addict. I didn't want people to know that I was a "crack baby". I got tired of my family only telling me that she was a great fighter but they refuse to tell me what a good mother she was or whether she cared about me or my sisters or not. I had to learn those details from my dad. There were many times I cried because I had no mother around when all my cousins did. Although my aunts never really could take the credit for raising their kids, they were still physically there. They could still pick their kids up when they finished doing whatever they were doing.

They could still watch their kids open presents on Christmas and prepare their girls for the prom. When I got old enough I finally realized that my mother (grandmother) was not my real mother. Where was she? I can't remember anything about her. I didn't know what her smiled looked like. I can't remember what her kiss or touch felt like. I don't remember me sitting between her legs while she dressed my hair and because a man stole my mother from me I will never be able to share my secrets, fears and accomplishments with her. God, had to know these things, how couldn't He when I've been taught that He knows all things. Why would God take her away? Why didn't He see that we needed her more? Why? Why? Why? I was taught never to question God, but I wanted answers and I *demanded* Him to answer. Wow! Demanded. Who was I to demand God?

Who was I to question the life He created? He had a right to take what He made, didn't He? After all He is the one that gives life so He should be able to have the authority to take it away. Shouldn't He? But God you have already taken from me...(That's what my mind and heart screamed aloud). See, back then I had an idea of who God was. I read the Bible, but didn't fully understand it. I heard the preacher discussing who God is and His capabilities, but I didn't fully comprehend. Since I was a little girl, I have always had a burning desire to know God. I enjoyed going to church, just to get an understanding of who He was. Deep down, I knew God loved me, but at the moment I couldn't face the One who I thought was the blame for my pain. All I knew He had taken yet another mother from me. I was angry with my grandmother because I felt that she could have fought a little harder. I was too selfish to realize that she'd been in pain almost all of her life.

I couldn't see that she was strictly tired and ready to go home where she could be at peace. No! I was livid! I was hurt beyond repair. How could you leave me at the prime of my life?After all I'd cleaned the house, made sure you were taken care of when your own children didn't have time for you. I'd made sure my sister and all my cousins and great cousins were okay when their mothers dropped them off without asking. I'd cooked for you, bathe you, fed you and loved you. Wasn't everything I did enough? Don't you know how much I love you? Why couldn't you see that I needed you more? Why would you give up, knowing that your children (my sisters and I) had nobody else in the world to care for us? Why? How? Why? Who was I to bring up the things I've done for her when she'd done so much for me that I wouldn't be able to pay her back?

Why couldn't I realized that she was an angel placed in my life just to care for me and my sister and God knew she was tired and was ready to come home? If only I could see that then but I couldn't. I was angry with myself for being angry with my grandmother and God. How could I be angry with God? I should have known that my anger was directed towards the wrong person. She'd lived her life and did great deeds. Everyone who knew her knew that she was sent by God. Whatever she could do for a person she would do. She opened her house to the homeless and would give all she could to help someone else. Then after awhile I focused on myself and realized I was only angry with me. I was angry because I felt that I didn't do enough for her or tell her that I loved her enough. I was angry because I never got a chance to tell her goodbye. I felt cheated and I felt that I deserved to tell my own mother goodbye. How dare God take her from me without me saying it and how dare she take her last breath without her hearing me say it and how dare me...

I should have said it more while she was living. There was this poem I read called Chosen One by Heather Will that just flowed through me and I could have sworn that it was written just for me:

Why did you take her? I cried to God.

He said, she wasn't yours to keep.

But why her? Why did you have to choose her?

Quietly I plead.

I did choose her, but I also chose you, His answer boldly came.

I don't understand, I replied.

And He answered me once again; I needed a mother for an Angel. Not just any person would do.

I needed someone with strength of heart, and courage beyond compare.

I needed someone I could rely on who wouldn't be afraid to care.

A person that sees beyond the pain, and understands the hurt.

To be a mother to an Angel is the grandest of My work.

I saw in you, all these things. You were perfect for the job.

I didn't know quite what to say, and all I could do was sob.

Don't cry, My child, I know this is hard, but it's all a part of My plan.

I've been with you along the way, I've never stopped holding your hand.

This job is tough and not meant to be easy, even now that My Angel is home.

And you've made Me so proud to see how in faith and love you have grown. I will always be near and you have a special place, for becoming a mother to an Angel of grace.

My heart became still, my mind was at peace; the answer had become clear.

I finally understood it all; the reason I was here.

Thank You, God for seeing in me what I could not see.

Your will is done and my service to You, will never stop.

And God said, I know...

The moral of this poem was God took an Angel out of my life to bring another into it. My grandmother lived to see me grow up from an infant to a young lady. Everything that I did for her prepared me for the life ahead of me. I'd grew up at an early age and I'm glad because it prepared me in more ways than one. Everything that I went through prepared me for the person I was destined to become in the future. Taking care of my grandmother and everything around the house not only taught me how to keep a clean house but also equipped me for my Angel that I have to raise and care for. Through it all God is letting me know even though it won't be easy He will always be there to help me. I thought I lost the only person I could ever prove my love to. I thought I'd lost my motivation and my reason for succeeding, but God saw it differently. God had prepared me for my own child. He'd given me the ability to learn all those qualities and which I learned to take into my parenthood.

He'd given me someone who I can show my love to and who would motivate me to succeed. He'd replaced my Angel for another one. It made perfect sense to me and although I was no longer angry, I was very sad. I didn't get to grieve when she died. I wrote a poem for her that I planned to recite at the funeral but as I stood up to speak I couldn't get the words out. I didn't get to say my farewell at the burial site because I'd fainted when they closed the casket. I was at Tift Regional Medical Center getting medical attention during the time that every one said their final goodbyes. It seemed too final. I wasn't prepared for all that. When I was younger I always said I would have liked to have died before she did because I didn't know if I would be able to take it if she left me. It's funny how you can underestimate the strength within you.

To this day I dream about her. At one point I would dream about her every night and it would feel like she wasn't even gone. In a way I was holding on to her for my own reasons. I didn't want to let her go and I didn't want to have to deal with the fact that she wasn't alive. I wanted her to keep living, even if it was only in my dreams. It took me to the year 2010 to accept that fact that she was gone I was finally able to let her go. I was finally able to accept that she was gone and if I wanted to see her again I better keep living for Jesus. She was the best mother in the world and although she'd had a stroke and couldn't do much, she did the best she could. There was never a Christmas when we didn't have boxes of presents, my bed was always warm and I never went to bed hungry. I wasn't rich, but I can't say that we were poor either. She couldn't do all of what we wanted but she did more then what we needed her to do. She was a warrior and what I would call my angel that God had sent down from heaven just to take care of me.

I was able to forgive myself because I understand that it was nothing that I could do and everything that I did for her spoke volumes. She already know I love her, she said so in my dreams. I feel better now because I was finally able to say goodbye. I finally was able to release her and release myself from all the pint up stuff that I'd held for so long. I'd just forgiven myself. I will not tell someone something that I have not learned myself. I know what it feels to be forgiven, to forgive others and to forgive myself. Now I am given you a bit of advice, now that you have forgiven that person, now forgive YOUSELF. It is harder for us to forgive ourselves then to forgive someone else. We have seen the power of forgiving someone else, but many struggle with blame, guilt and the inability to forgive ourselves.

Picture it... May 17th 1998, the first tragedy that ever blew me to pieces. That day was one of the worst days of my life, maybe the worst. I know you are probably saying my life was filled with tragedies, we all have a story to tell but life for me ain't been no crystal stair. I still have flashbacks of the day and I use to think I was constantly living in a nightmare that I couldn't wake up from. I had to be about 10 years old at the time, Zen, better known as Scooter was 11 and Abrian was about 8 or 9, but anyway we (including my sister Audrianna and four other cousins) ended up at what we called "the waterfall" which was nothing more then an area surrounded by trees, water cascading from the rocks that fell down into some deep, dirty water. We knew we weren't supposed to go there and as we were heading that way a feeling hit me and I felt the need to turn around.

I expressed my feelings to Scooter but he insisted that we go. Back then I was like a tomboy and a dare devil I only went because Scooter called me scary. So, I shook off the feeling and I remember us going further into some woods with prickly trees because I kept getting pricked by them. Since Scooter and I were the oldest we felt responsible for the younger kids warning them to play around the base of the water and not to go any further. We all took off our clothes because we knew we'd get a beating if our clothes got wet. As we were playing we heard a scream coming towards the water. It was my sister, screaming help. She'd gone out in the water. We all thought she was just playing around and we laughed but when her head kept going under the water we knew she wasn't playing. Scooter and I looked at each other and quickly jumped into the water to get her.

Now Scooter was a way better swimmer than I was but while we were in the water even he panicked. We couldn't see a thing in that water and all we could do was keep swimming as we held on to each others hand. We couldn't locate my sister and for a while we just struggled in the water together, both of us trying to stay above water, until I felt a pain in my hand as if I'd been bitten. I jerked my hand back so fast that I'd let go of Scooter hand. As soon as I'd let it go I quickly tried to grab it again but all I grabbed was water. I don't know how long I tried to find him but after a while I begin to feel a sense of loss. I knew he was gone. Just like I knew that I would soon be gone as well. I didn't fight it; I just accepted it, closed my eyes, prayed to God and released myself. Now, I know some people don't believe in miraculous powers or anything like that, but that could be because they'd never experienced the hands of God.

I don't know how... I don't know when and I don't know why, but when I opened my eyes I was on solid ground. Later my sister told me that my cousin Abrian got me out of the water with a stick. Now whether I held on to the stick I do not know. I do not remember any of it. I laid there for a while trying to get myself together when something hit me. *Scooter.* I looked around asking everybody where he was and nobody said anything, they were just crying. My sister was out of the water, I later found out that one of my cousins, Fred, helped her out. I don't know how but I got up enough energy to get up and I was okay. Scooter was nowhere to be seen. After a neighborhood friend tried to help find Scooter to no avail, I went to go get help. I don't know where the strength came from but I ran all the way to my aunt house nonstop. She was just cutting up some greens in a pot when I told her.

I don't even remember telling her where we was all I can remember is that she dropped the pot of greens and ran. I then spotted a police officer at the light; he must have thought I was crazy. There I was a scared, wet and nappy headed little something banging on his window like my life depended on it. My life might have not depended on it but Scooter's did. I told him that my cousin had drowned and I showed him where we were at, then after I showed him I ran home and burst in the door crying and screaming. I remember my cousin Shamorra and my grandmother being there when I told them that Scooter was dead. They thought I was playing until I got really hysterical. Then I remember Shamorra picking up the phone only to find out that Abrian had jumped in to try to save Scooter and drowned too. Nothing prepared me for that hit. It felt like someone had punched me in my chest. My mind was like a whirlwind and I could have sworn the walls were closing in on me. The following day people came in with comfort and I tried so hard to comfort my aunt Pam (Scooter's mom). I couldn't possibly know what it was like for neither of my aunts. Each one had lost their only child. All I know is that I felt numb and at a complete lost. It was like I was there but I wasn't there. All I wanted to do was crawl up in a corner and die. I didn't understand, why. Why spare me at the risk of losing two cousins? Why take Scooter and not me when after all we'd both been in the water together? When I had the feeling about not going there in the beginning, why didn't I listen to the warning? I wanted to take Abrian's place because I felt that it should have been me and not him. If only I would have not let go of Scooter hand then this would all never happened. If only I didn't leave them alone, then Abrian would still be alive.

I had constant nightmares and it took me years to live with the fact that they were gone. It took me even longer to forgive myself for what I felt was my fault. I no longer had nightmares but dreams about them with smiles on their faces. I knew then that they were happy and then I was able to release them. I'd held on to the nightmares for too long it was time to release myself. I'd let go of the guilt, the pain and the shame. I no longer felt that I was to blame but I believed that God thought that it would be better if they were with Him. I realized that it was not my fault and I had did all I could do. Do you feel responsible for something that caused pain to someone else? Did you cheat on your spouse or significant other? Did you abuse someone? Did you quit school? Have a baby at a young age and out of wedlock? Did you break the law? No matter what you're feeling or the situation whether big or small, if you can't forgive yourself then you can't move on with your life.

We have all made mistakes in our lives that we often hold against ourselves. Give yourself a break! You're not perfect. We have all done things that are not pleasing. Do not imprison yourself; release those chains from your mind. In order to learn something, we have to go through some things. If the mistakes you've made and the trials and tribulations taught you something more than you knew before than it could have been a test you had to face in order to prepare you. Since I gave my life over to Christ and began to evaluate my self I begin to understand the power of forgiveness. For a while I was holding on to past pains and making up excuses of why I did what I did. I was still chained to pains that I either didn't know how to let go or refuse to let go. The pain that Jim caused, pain that my mother caused, pain that my family caused, pain that my ex's caused, pain that my so-called friends caused and the pain I caused myself.

It's funny how a person can hold on to stuff for so long while the other person has moved on with no clue that you still feel a certain way about them. One day I connected with Jim on Facebook and I wrote him a long letter asking him to forgive me and explaining why I'd forgiven myself. I asked him to forgive me for expecting more out of him then he was willing to give and I told him that I'd forgiven him for taking advantage of the love he knew I had for him. I asked him to forgive me for pushing myself on him and practically trying to force him to love me and I told him that I'd forgiven myself for failing to love myself enough. There was a lot I specified that I will not elaborate on, mostly because I don't remember all of it. Anyway, I thanked him for being honest with me because if it wasn't for that day in Florida I wouldn't have ever known what true love felt like. I would have never been able to explain how it felt to be held by God.

I wouldn't have ever known that all along there was a man of great power that could love me better than any mortal man in this world. God healed me from the pain as I tapped the keys on my computer, forgiving the man that I'd thought wronged me, when I only wronged myself. God helped me realize that I only needed Him all along; that even though I'd put another before Him, He was still there, waiting on me to come back to my first true love. He never gave up on me. He help me to realize that all though I'd felt forsaken by Jim, He would never and could never do me like that. Jim forgave me and wondered why I wrote it. I told him I had to release myself and move on; that I wouldn't be able to move on unless I got that off my chest. I must have lost my mind, loving someone more than I loved me. I must have forgotten how valuable I was and that I didn't need a man to validate my value. For some clueless reason I thought he could be the one to make me feel butterflies, to feel complete and happy. I was mistaken.

I had simply mistaken myself. I had to free myself from the past afflictions that had an affect on my love life. I had to set him free without him realizing that he needed to be free. Free from me. Free from the love that I still held for him and the hatred that I still carried all the same. Its funny how you can be caught up in one man/woman and years later wonder what in the world you were going through during that time. I have always said "never do something that you're ashamed of and never regret a mistake that has increased your wisdom and made you grow." Some people say, "If I knew then what I knew now I would have..." or "I wish I could turn back time I never would have done..." In my opinion, you would have done the exact same thing that you did before. Back then you didn't have the knowledge of understanding your mistake but because you experienced the outcome you now know what the results led to. How else would you have known?

Stop complaining about the mistakes you have made and think about the positive side of it all. Learn how to discern the truth of your own actions. Stop blaming others for your own actions! Let go of the past! Stop dictating your mistakes and life choices on what somebody did to you long ago. You have the ability to change everything in your life. When you get a certain age, you have control over who you are, what you became and what you do. We tend to play the victim all the time, rather than examine ourselves. What you do and say to others affects your situation. Yes, your words, actions and attitudes are most likely the blame for your situation. You got fired, not because of what your mother, father, uncle, sister, brother, or the "white man" did to you in the past, but because of what you did. Own up to the things you do! Lean on God to gain the wisdom and insight of persecution that He offer to us. When persecution occurs because of your own fault, God encourages us all to seek forgiveness and change our wrongful ways.

Your mother or father may not have always been in your life to teach you or help direct your path, but you can take that same neglect and reverse it into something positive. When you have kids, you can take what you've learned and be able to be a better parent then your parent(s) were because you already know how it feels to be parentless. Yeah, I may have had a child at a young age and out of wedlock, but in the end, that same child motivated me to go towards my dreams. Over the years I have learned to be more patient, self-disciplined and I have my priorities in order. Now look at how what I felt was a huge mistake turn out to be my blessing. So, if your mistakes have caused you to be a better person, embrace that mistake and share it with someone who has gone through or is going through the same situation as you.

You never know how your life story can help someone else. We are troubled on every side, yet not distressed; we are perplexed, but not in despair; persecuted, but not forsaken; cast down, but not destroyed (2 Corinthians 4:8-9)." People also will persecute you for doing all the right things. Consider yourself blessed when somebody does that to you. That just gives you the indication that everything that you are doing in life is right. Ask God, to help you see the things you are doing and give you the wisdom to separate persecution because of your own faults and persecution because of your commitment to Him. To be able to forgive is so powerful that everything in you starts transforming and it shows on the outside as well. When you forgive you learn to be more acceptable and trusting. You will not learn the art of self-discipline or build faith unless you are able to forgive yourself for all those time you've failed to be accepting, trusting and faithful. Understand that unless you're able to forgive yourself, everything else will falter. You will not be able to forgive anyone for treating you wrong and inadequately until you are willing to forgive yourself for treating yourself wrong.

Yes, you have disappointed yourself. You have treated yourself any kind of way and did yourself wrong. You have made promises to yourself that you couldn't keep. You have put aside your hopes and dreams to satisfy another. You have forgotten what it was like to be purposeful and independent. You have set yourself aside, abandoning you when you needed you the most. Then you wonder why you end up with friends and in relationships with those who end up treating you wrong and are not giving you the adequate amount of attention, love and affection that you need. You wonder why they disappoint you, act mean to you, belittle you, make promises that they don't keep, abandon you, reject you, use and abuse you. It is not because of what they are doing, it is because of what you have been doing to yourself. It's because of what you accept and what you feel you deserve.

It's because of the effects of your failure to make yourself accountable and forgiving yourself. You have to learn to be good to yourself. Love you enough to forgive yourself, so when people come into your life you will be able to identify the good with the bad. You will no longer accept the little things people offer you and you would begin finding someone who feels the same way you feel about yourself because you want have it no other way.

The Seven Pillars of Forgiveness

"Blessed are the merciful, for they shall obtain mercy."
~Matthew 5:7

The Seven Pillars of Forgiveness

3

*F*ORGIVENESS IS THE most important thing you can give to yourself and others. It opens up new windows that you have sealed closed for so long. Everything about you begins to change and you see yourself turning a new leaf and see a different view of things that you didn't see before. One of the best things I did for myself was to be able to forgive and let go. There was weight lifted off my shoulders and I felt so much better. had a hold on me because I'd taken my power back. When I was in the state of unforgiveness I didn't want to forgive, I wanted to be in full control only to realize that I was being controlled. The unforgiveness I held on to held me captive and so did the memories.

Even as I forgave I still held on to the memory, I had to release myself from those memories, because as long as I held on to those memories the pain was only refreshing. I've humbled myself and acknowledge the hurt that I'd afflicted upon myself and had allowed others to afflict on me as well. I am at peace with me and have grown from a girl into a woman. Forgiveness allows us to see things in a completely different perspective. I have come up with my own seven pillars of forgiveness that I feel will benefit you when it comes to forgiving yourself and others. These pillars explain what forgiveness can give to you if you allow yourself to forgive. These pillars are: Understanding, Healing, Mental and Spiritual Freedom, Inner Peace, Growth, Humility and Power.

PILLAR ONE: UNDERSTANDING

First and foremost, you have to first understand a person and why they do what they do. Sometimes we just write people off without allowing them to explain. You have to be able to get to the root of the problem in order to find out what type of seed is implanted. Some people just do what they do because that's just who they are and what they know. I always say, "You can't get mad at a person, if they show you who they are. Either you accept them or leave them alone." You know what to expect out of those who reveal themselves to you, it's those who don't that you have to worry about. But then there are some people who deal with things in their life that play a major part in their actions and behaviors. Understand that nobody is perfect and we all make mistakes in life. The Bible say in Luke 17:3-4, "Pay attention to yourselves! If your brother sins, rebuke him, and if he repents, forgive him, and if he sins against you seven times in the day, and turns to you seven times, saying, 'I repent,' you must forgive him."

Just like you would want someone else to forgive you for an act that was unpleasing then you should be able to offer the next person the same thing. You also have to understand that everyone that comes into your life is not always good for you. We have all came across people who have done something hurtful to us. It's all about learning and experiencing. We will never know who and who not to have in our space, if we don't experience. In some cases the person that you ask to forgive you will, but if they don't then at least you did your part. Seeking forgiveness from another is not always about them accepting it, it's about you taking the step to want to forgive or obtaining forgiveness to find inner peace. You may not even always understand why a person do what they do but understanding open up the door for you so you can be able to walk into a newer and more forgiving you.

It took me awhile to understand why my past relationships ended in the way that they did. It took me even longer to understand that I was the key player in every aspect of my life. As a child I couldn't fully control what people did to me but as I grew older I was able to make choices in my life and I chose to love Jim, just like I chose to love Terrell. The outcome of those relationships ended and began because of my approval. What Jim did to me was not to hurt me intentionally but because I did not won't to accept what he was saying or see it from his point of view I took what he said and made it into something that it wasn't. I understand that what I had to go through with Jim was actually for the best. Terrell and I jumped head first in our relationship from day one.

We made rash decisions, without fully thinking things through. I was hearing wedding bells before I knew what his favorite color was. When time past, different and realistic thoughts begin to set in and I had to make some tough but necessary decisions when it came to our relationship. I'd mix something seasonal with lifetime expectations. We have to learn to live and let go of those things that are not apart of our future and it's hard to do that if you've told yourself that, that person is your future. If you understand that the pain you went through could be a lesson you had to learn to grow then you will be able to begin the healing process.

Forgiveness does not change the past but it changes the pain of the past and unlocks the door to the future. ~*Unknown*

PILLAR TWO: HEALING

The healing process could be the hardest part you have to face. The hurt, the pain and the brokenness that you feel when someone has done something so tragic to you disables you, breaks you down and mentally and spiritually takes pieces and pieces of you until you're unidentifiable. You may feel like there is nothing left to give because you have given so much. There are never healing scars and wombs that have been afflicted in you that never stops bleeding. You must concentrate on the act of forgiving, not on the situation or circumstance behind why you are trying to forgive. The best place to start in the healing process is admitting. You have to admit that you are hurt. Feel the hurt. Cry, yell or scream. Do whatever you have to do to release yourself. You have to be able to face those who hurt you, face those you hurt and face yourself.

It's okay to be upset, sad or angry but do not meditate on that pain indefinitely. When you continue to relive the pain that you went through, you're reopening the wound over and over again and if that wound stays open long enough an infection may occur. You have to get in a place where you have to face the pain, go through that pain and take the proper steps in healing. In James 5:15-16 says, "And the prayer of faith shall save the sick, and the Lord shall raise him up; and if he has committed sins, they shall be forgiven him. Confess your faults one to another, and pray one for another, that you may be healed. The effectual fervent prayer of a righteous man avails much." You have to be able to release all of the access waste out of your body or it will settle and cause health problems to occur. All of that pint up frustration can really affect you. Bottled up anger only makes you bitter and doesn't anybody want to be around a bitter person.

All the unforgiveness you have carried could bring on headaches, high blood pressure, different stressors, heart attacks, cancer and a lot of other medical problems. Many people do not realize how harboring pain can cause problems internally. Forgiveness may not be able cure cancer, but it releases hatred, stress and anger which can really improve your emotional, spiritual and physical health. You have to take yourself through a cleansing phase detoxifying all those toxic poisons up out of your body. Your heart begins to heal and love will have an opportunity of coming in. It may take you more time to forgive then others and it is nothing wrong with that as long as you have the intention of one day forgiving. There is nothing wrong with you; you just need more love and more time to heal.

It always helps to talk to someone who you know will give you good council but I would first recommend that you talk to God. He is everything that you will need in the end. I knew that I'd finally healed and forgiven when I was able to actually gain a friendship with my ex's and give them advice on relationships and about their current relationships. You will know if you've healed because that very person that caused you pain can walk past you and you can speak. You can tell them that you wish them well and truly mean it from the bottom of your heart.

All healing is first a healing of the heart. ~J.R.R. Tolkien

PILLAR THREE MENTAL & SPIRITUAL FREEDOM

Forgiveness does not mean that you are giving people the authorization to treat you any kind of way. It is a favor to yourself to allow your mind and your spirit to be freed from the bondage of unforgiveness. It teaches you different steps which give you the ability to make different approaches in a situation. You become more aware of what you will and will not accept or take from others. When you release all those past toxins (hate, fear, anger, resentment, guilt, strife, and shame), it clears you mind and your thought process. You are now able to think clearly. You have the freedom and the authority to choose what you allow to bother you. This means that fear, hate, anger and all those things can only settle inside of you if you allow them to. You have the freedom to make a decision whether you will allow others words and actions to affect you. Mind over matter.

Those that mind do not matter and those that matter does not mind. Think about the operation of cause and affect. If you don't consider or think about the cause, then it is impossible for there to be an effect. By choosing to forgive, negative thoughts and emotions cannot create a negative effect. Forgiveness will help you spiritually because the willingness to not forgive has an effect on how you walk with God. Philippians 2:2-4 says, "Complete my joy by being of the same mind, having the same love, being in full accord and of one mind. Do nothing from rivalry or conceit, but in humility count others more significant than yourselves. Let each of you look not only to his own interests, but also to the interests of others." How can you walk rightfully with God with hatred and unforgiveness in your heart? The Bible teaches us about forgiveness and love. Forgiveness gives you the spiritual freedom you need to go to another level with God. Once you are mentally and spiritually free, a sense of peace over takes you in a way you've never felt before.

Stand fast therefore in the liberty wherewith Christ hath made us free, and be not entangled again with the yoke of bondage." ~ *Galatians 5:1*

PILLAR FOUR: INNER PEACE

I've had conversations with many people who live their lives surrounded around what they have done to someone or what someone has done to them; they are completely consumed by it. Have you ever been around a person who constantly talks about what someone did to them and how they could never forgive them? What people fail to realize is that when unforgiveness eat away at you, it takes away your peace. The longer it takes you to forgive the longer you will stay connected to those who hurt you. Your thoughts will constantly rewind to the part of the scene in your mind of that person and what they did to you. Over and over again it will replay in your mind and that emotional link between you and that person can be so strong that it causes inner tumult. Forgiveness releases you from that turmoil that overcrowds your state of mind, your emotions and of course, your peace. When you find it in your heart to forgive them you can find your peace.

Inner peace can be reached only when we practice forgiveness. Forgiveness is letting go of the past, and is therefore the means for correcting our misperceptions." ~ *Gerald Jampolsky*

PILLAR FIVE: GROWTH

Forgiving someone and/or asking someone to forgive you, shows your level of maturity. Some people don't forgive because of their pride. "Pride goes before destruction, and a haughty spirit before a fall (Proverbs 16:18)." When you look beyond your pride you begin to grow in wisdom. Your love for others grows and so does your faith in God increase as well as your walk with God. People will be able to look at you and not even recognize who you are and those who have known you will say, "Yes, this is the person I remember, welcome back."

PILLAR SIX: HUMILITY

With all that mess out of your system that resulted from forgiveness you are now able to get you some humility. You will find yourself more at ease and more polite to others. Your attitude changes and so does your personality. You become more humble and open to new possibilities. God's grace is healing and through forgiveness He gives heals us. When we receive forgiveness we learn of humility and what it really means to feel unworthy. When we are able to give forgiveness, we learn about grace and what it really feels like to be released.

"Therefore all things whatsoever ye would that men should do to you, do ye even so to them: for this is the law and the prophets." ~*Matthew 7:12*

PILLAR SEVEN: POWER

Forgiveness gives you your power back. The person you have forgiven no longer has the power to invade in your thoughts and have a negative affect on you. You are now powerful enough to move forward with your life and take full control. At some point you have to make a decision to move forward and not allow what happen to you to take full control over your life. Acknowledge that it happened, make an effort to find some kind of peace and move on. When you meet people who have forgiven, you see their power. It's the way they walk into a room or the way they talk and/or it could be the way that they handle a situation. Eye for an eye does not give you power it only make things worse. Forgiveness is good. When I learned to forgive I noted how much I've healed and now I am able to tell someone else how to forgive, whether you forgive the person or not is up to you, but just know that you are hurting yourself more than you are hurting the other person. The best thing you can do is forgive. The best defeat is to be able to forgive a person who has wronged you. Love is power! Peace is power! Forgiveness is power!

It's In Your Mind

"If you could change your mindset, then you can change your life."
~Kezia Davis

It's In Your Mind

4

*H*AVE YOU EVER wondered why you had a sudden thought about something that was against everything that you believed in? Have you ever thought about wanting something so bad that you start feeling that you need it and then your feelings tells you that you got to have it then all of sudden you feel like you love it so much that you just can't be without it? That's because the way you think can speak to your feelings and your feelings speaks to the heart.

I've learned that when God speaks He doesn't leave you confused nor will He speak anything to you that is not connected to His Word. Be consistent with asking God to renew your mind and be cautious as to what you let flow through your mind and who you you allow speak into you. Not everyone is right with God and some who claims that God speaks to them is questionable. So that is why it is important to test every spirit. The devil causes trouble on every side and if he can't get to your heart he will definitely try to get to your mind and if he can get to your mind, then he will have the freedom to consistently wreak havoc and speak sinful things into it. The mind is so powerful that the Bible says, "it is with the mind that we serve the Lord." That's why the enemy battles with you inside your mind. All he has to do is chain your mind to keep you bound with unvarying worry, tension, provocation, low self-esteem and hostility.

He can plant a type of sickness within the mind that leave you physically sick. It's the devil's job to cause separation between God's people. 1 Peter 5:8 warns us to "Be sober, be vigilant; because your adversary the devil, as a roaring lion, walketh about, seeking whom he may devour." The devil don't stop his job that's why you have to constantly pray and keep God on your speed dial. Don't give the devil any leverage. As soon as he see's even the smallest unoccupied space within you he will try to take its vacancy. "Do not be conformed to this world, but be transformed by the renewing of your mind, that you may prove what is good and acceptable and perfect will of God (Romans 12:2)." Spiritual transformation starts in the mind and heart. A mind that is dedicated to the world and its concerns will produce a life tossed back and forth by the currents of the world and our culture. But a mind dedicated to God's truth will produce a life that can stand the test of time.

We can resist the temptations of our culture by meditating on God's truth and letting the Holy Spirit guide and shape our thoughts and behaviors (Romans 12:2 Amplified). In T.D. Jakes sermon titled "Free Your Mind", he explains the verse by saying, "Don't shape yourself around the comings and goings of this world. Don't shape your opinions and attitudes around circumstances that you cannot change. Don't build your identity around worldliness." Be ye transformed— this means to put on another form put away your old self, change your sinful nature to righteous behavior. By the renewing—change how you view things and the way you feel. If you can get your mind out of those chains, then you can get your health, prosperity and everything else that the devil has held captive out. If only you can break those chains no devil in hell would be able to stop you from staying free. No weapon.

Jump out head first and everything that is connected to your head will follow. Cast that devil down and let him know that you have no room for the stupidity. The devil is so persistent that he will keep coming back to see how far he can go with you. That is why you have to keep the Word planted inside the fragments of your heart. You have to speak the Word to him with authority. Look at how many times he tried to tempt Jesus in the wilderness, but Jesus constantly threw the Word at Him until he eventually gave up and fled, but that didn't stop him from finding a way to get to Jesus. The devil jumped into Judas Iscariot and cause Judas to betray God for thirty pieces of silver, but Jesus still got the victory in the end. The devil still couldn't touch him. Again, if you can change your mind, you can change your life. Some of you are so far behind time in our mind that it's clear why you feel defeated.

The reason you're dealing with any defeat in your life is because you haven't linked up your mind with your heart. You have the authority to speak to your feelings, tell your feelings how to feel. Retrain your mind on how to think. In the King James Version of the Bible it says, "whatsoever things are true, whatsoever things are honest, whatsoever things are just, whatsoever things are pure, whatsoever things are lovely, whatsoever things are of good report; if there be any virtue, and if there be any praise, think on these things." You have the authority to speak life unto you. I tell myself every morning that I wake up, "this is the day that the Lord has made and I will rejoice and be glad in it. I refuse to allow anyone or anything to steal my joy today. I will not entertain idiocy and the devil will not have the luxury of getting on my nerves. So as a man thinketh so is he. So, Kezia, you are blessed beyond measure. You are healthy, smart, loved, highly favored, and wanted. Why? Because God said so and I say so." "He said that I was the head and not the tail and I was His child and I have a place in His kingdom; therefore I am royalty. I have peace and can't anybody take it. I reign in victory. What I'm going through is not as bad as what I could be going through." Speak into your circumstances, speak into your situation. Believe in what thus says the Lord and know what God can do. You have got to have the mind to change. Ask God to give you a new perspective. Change the way you perceive things and free your mind from all negativity. Some of you are stuck in the situation you're in because of your mindset. Some of you can't get ahead because you so busy looking in the rear view mirror (what's behind you) instead of looking through the mirror in front of you (what's a head). Cause if you keep looking back in the rear view mirror, you will not be able see what's ahead, therefore, causing a head-on collision.

Some of you are stuck at the same job that you are unhappy in, because you are afraid to step out and take a risk that could drive you into your career. You'd rather work in a place of total discomfort just to make ends meet, then to move forward to your greatest potential. Then you want to complain and make up excuses. Who have tainted your mind to the point where you have become hindered in their opinion of you. You do not pursue your education because someone has convinced to believe that you are not smart enough and they have told you that you will never amount to anything in your life.

You must speak into the lie that was told to you. Speak against every negative thing that is hindering you to get to the next level. Then there are some who hold on to unhealthy, dysfunctional, and unsuccessful relationships because they have tricked themselves into believing that, he or she is the best thing that you can do. He has told you that you can't do no better than him, and that he is the only one who wants you. He has told you that you are ugly, fat, stupid, and useless. You settle because you'd rather have a piece of something than nothing at all. You'd rather have someone to lay beside every other night (depending on when he/she wants to come home), then come home to an empty bed. You are not self-fulfilled. Understand that if you can't be happy with yourself and by yourself then you will never understand the essence of true happiness. You will never understand that as long as you have Jesus you're never alone. Some of you are so stuck and so connected to the things of this world that in your mind you can't possibly think beyond the heavenly realm. You're okay with having just enough. You don't mind staying on government assistance. You accept the fact that life can't get any better for you. You want more but you don't have the mind to do more. You're stuck in a miserable place because you don't have the mind to think beyond anything else. Some of you constantly complain about no privacy, no peace and wanting something of your own, but because you are afraid to get out of your comfort zone you deal with your surroundings, you complain.

Some of you still live with your parents or whoever is taking care of you, because of fear of struggling. You fear not having enough or having to work hard to get what you need. Stuff has been given to you for too long. You don't have to worry about paying a bill at mama house. You don't have to worry about eating at grandma's house. You don't have to worry about spending your own money at Henry house because they are supplying it all. You ready to go when mama don't want you coming in all times of the night, you want to be out on your own when grandma refuse to let Henry sleep over night in her house. You want your space and to let Henry go when he isn't giving you what you want; when he finally ask you to go to work; when he's beating on you; when he starts sleeping with every Nancy, Susie and Karen on you; when he decides to share Angela, Isis, Debra and Susan (AIDS) or Stephanie, Tiffany and Diana (STD) with you or maybe he decides to share Hector, Ivan and Vance (HIV) he don't discriminate.

Especially when Nancy decides that she won't raise her baby and leave Jada on your front door step and the icing is put on the cake when Henry expects you to play mommy and help take care of Jada. Some of you accept all of the above and still live with mama, grandma and Henry, but you complain about feeling like you're in prison and being shackled. You feel shackled and in bondage because you've set your mind up to believe those things. You've accepted the cards that you've dealt to yourself and forever losing. You are not free because you do not realize the power you have to change your situation. You could have been free a long time ago. Get out of the familiarity, step out of your comfort zone and break out of the fear that you've allowed to overtake you. Stop holding on to old stuff, let it go. Stop bringing it up, it should have been forgotten. Stop looking for answers from other people.

Stop looking for a handout; nobody is going to give you anything especially if you're not making the effort in obtaining it yourself. You're not a child anymore... When I was a child, I spoke as a child, I understood as a child, I thought as a child, but when I became a woman, I put away childish things. Nobody was coming to rescue me. I had to help myself. When I finally decided that in order to obtain the things I wanted I must first have the mentality to go out there in get it. Nothing is free in this world. There was nobody out there that was going to give me anything. I had responsibilities to take of and I had to be the one to complete them. Yes, I decided that marijuana and alcohol was not the answer, but a poison, that I called "my medicine", that didn't cure me, but only deepen the sickness. When I realized that senseless fighting and cursing resolved nothing... When I actually sat down and realized that I didn't need anyone to tell me how pretty I am, or how smart and sexy I was or that I didn't need friends to feel apart of a crowd, reader... that was when I grew up.

When are you going to put the childish things behind you and become an adult? Get rid of that old mindset. All the unforgiveness, all the pettiness, all the bitterness, all pride, the past, the mind of thinking that everything should go your way, the mind of thinking that everyone should care about what you care about, care about how you think and how you feel. Get over it sweetheart, everybody isn't going to care as much as the next. Everybody isn't worried about what you think, how you feel and what you do. Everybody isn't concerned about how you dress, what you look like and what you got going on in your house. Everybody isn't against you and you don't give them the opportunity to be against you because you're too busy being against yourself. Stop entertaining the mess, move on and grow up. I'm asking again, DO YOU HAVE THE MIND TO CHANGE? Until you have the mind to change then everything around you will remain the same.

You Can Be Your Own Hindrance

"You want help? Start by helping yourself." ~Common Sense

You Can Be Your Own Hindrance

5

*Y*OU CANNOT ALLOW the past to define your future. Failure is what you make of it and there is no restriction in life unless you create it. Accomplishments can only be succeeded if one go out and work towards it. Stop setting limitations on your life and go out and bring your dreams to life, even if it seems impossible. There is nothing too impossible if your faith is in the right place and your mind is fixated on the right goals. People can become their own hindrance. Like I said in the previous chapter... GET YOUR MIND RIGHT! It's all about you and the mind-set that you have. What you believe in your mind normally reflects your feelings and actions. So begin to think like you already got it and your actions will soon work its way into doing what you need to obtain it. Some people are too quick to settle, without realizing that possibilities are endless. Do you help yourself or hinder yourself when it comes to going after the things you want in life?

One of, a few of the regrets I have in life is that I didn't go after the things I wanted as vigorously as I should have. Except for my writing, I did not apply the energy and drive I should have. You want to be happy? Then help yourself to happiness. Tired of the job you're working at? Help yourself to a better job. Stop being so comfortable with just enough. And who said you had to accept what you got? When you feel you deserve more you go out and seek what you feel you deserve. Have you ever been around a person who complains about the situation that they are in over and over again? After time has past you get tired of hearing it and figure that they must love the life they live because they are still living it. When a person is really tired then they will know because they will start taking action. Take Ike and Tina Turner relationship for instance. Yes, I used them.

For years Ike had control over Tina's life and abused her both emotionally and physically. In the beginning he promised her much and gave her much but at what cost? After years and years of abuse, Tina was at a point of hopelessness. She realized that the only person that can help her was herself. She fought her way out of that relationship and is living today with her head held high. If she furthered her relationship with Ike it was no telling where she would be. A change in every aspect of your life has to shift. There comes a point in a person's life when they have to fight their way out of their circumstances. You are who you attract. If you are a diamond don't go out looking for a Cubic Zirconium (CZ) these two stones do not have the same quality, both are made up from different material. However, one can easily be mistaken for the other if you don't know the quality of the stones. They may have the same clear color that sparkles in the light, but under close inspection, you will discover that a diamond has more brilliance (sparkles) than a CZ.

But the truth remains the same; one is real with expensive quality and one is fairly cheap. You have to know the difference between the two or you can be fooled into buying the cheap stuff. You get what you accept and what you buy for that matter. Who you choose to be in a relationship with, who you choose as friends and the things you do in life can all be linked to who you are, what you attract and what you accept. You hinder yourself from having the right people in your circle. Don't expect a man or woman with no dreams or goals to accept yours or help you accomplish them. They wouldn't have any advice to give you nor will they be a positive role model for you. Often times, these types of people want to see you fail, because misery loves company and they don't want anyone to be more than what they are. Having a meaningless relationship is just like vinegar and oil.

In order to understand why oil and vinegar don't mix, you have to first understand their individual compositions. Vinegar has more water and oil has more lipids (fats). When you mix these two components together, the oil floats to the top. It is so much easier for water to blend with more water than for it to blend with oil. Surround yourself around people that love God. With people who are honest, independent, self-driven and hard-working. These types of people will always have positive advice to give and could help lead you in the right direction. Be around people that can tell you the truth without trying to appease your ego. The truth hurts sometimes and it's necessary and important to get it in you. They want to see you succeed; they sincerely love you and want to see you prosper. There is nothing like having someone in your life that is true to you, but first you have to be true to yourself. Know who you are! Be real with yourself! Stop letting people lie to you and stop lying to yourself. People tend to lie to themselves to make themselves feel better. You knew it was a lie when you said it to yourself. Why lie? I'll tell you why, because it's simply easy to do it.

If you lie then the pain of knowing won't surface. Your ego and emotions can remain in check. What you don't know want hurt you, right? Wrong! The very thing you don't know could be the very thing that kills you. You don't know where Charlie was and who he was with, but by you not knowing eat a way at your senses, killing your ego, breaking down your self-esteem and changing your sleeping and eating patterns. You know that Faith could have been sleeping with someone else while you were overseas and that baby she's carrying could not be yours. Some of you have a problem with discovering who you are, because you are afraid of what you will discover. Try looking in the mirror and admitting to yourself that you are not perfect. Embrace your imperfection and continue to work on yourself to a point where you feel good enough to tell the truth and stop holding on to the people, places, and things that are holding you back from doing what you are purposed to do.

T.D. Jakes never cease to amaze me. He helped me figure out that I had to really let some stuff go because I was hindering my own self from the blessings that God had for me. Let it go... Let it go... Let it go... He said: There are people who can walk away from you. And hear me when I tell you this! When people can walk away from you: let them walk. I don't want you to try to talk another person into staying with you, loving you, calling you, caring about you, coming to see you, staying attached to you. I mean hang up the phone. When people can walk away from you let them walk. Your destiny is never tied to anybody that left. The bible said that, they came out from us that it might be made manifest that they were not for us. For had they been of us, no doubt they would have continued with us (1 John 2:19). People leave you because they are not joined to you. And if they are not joined to you, you can't make them stay.

Let them go.

And it doesn't mean that they are a bad person it just means that their part in the story is over. And you've got to know when people's part in your story is over so that you don't keep trying to raise the dead. You've got to know when it's dead. You've got to know when it's over. Let me tell you something. I've got the gift of good-bye. It's the tenth spiritual gift, I believe in good-bye. It's not that I'm hateful, it's that I'm faithful, and I know whatever God means for me to have He'll give it to me. And if it takes too much sweat I don't need it. Stop begging people to stay.

Let them go!!

If you are holding on to something that doesn't belong to you and was never intended for your life, then you need to...

LET IT GO!!!

If you are holding on to past hurts and pains...

LET IT GO!!!

If someone can't treat you right, love you back, and see your worth...

LET IT GO!!!

If someone has angered you.

LET IT GO!!!

If you are holding on to some thoughts of evil and revenge...

LET IT GO!!!

If you are involved in a wrong relationship or addiction...

LET IT GO!!!

If you are holding on to a job that no longer meets your needs or talents

LET IT GO!!!

If you have a bad attitude.....

LET IT GO!!!

If you keep judging others to make yourself feel better...

LET IT GO!!!

If you're stuck in the past and God is trying to take you to a new level in Him...

LET IT GO!!!

If you are struggling with the healing of a broken relationship...

LET IT GO!!!

If you keep trying to help someone who won't even try to help themselves...

LET IT GO!!!

If you're feeling depressed and stressed...

LET IT GO!!!

If there is a particular situation that you are so used to handling yourself and God is saying 'take your hands off of it,' then you need to...
LET IT GO!!!
Let the past be the past. Forget the former things. GOD is doing new things for 2011!
Note: He said 2009, but I said 2011
LET IT GO!!!
Get Right or Get Left ... think about it, and then.
LET IT GO!!!
'The Battle is the Lord's!'
You can't fight a battle that you're not suited up for. You don't have the artillery or the man power to come against that war that you're facing. You have to show that you're doing something to help yourself so that people and God will be delighted in helping you. So folks, make ways to help yourself and God will help you. Don't you know that God can very well have your blessings tied up because of you and what you're holding on to? He want to release it to you but you're too busy following behind Frank and holding on to Kimberly that you have no room for the blessings that God has for you. You're too comfortable or too afraid to move out that house or that environment you are in that He can't house you in your new home that could be in another state. The fear...Let it go! The hurt...Let it go! The pain that you've self afflicted on yourself... Let it go! That alcohol, the drugs, the prescription pills, the cigarettes, the fatty foods and all that stuff you're addicted to will not fulfill your most inner need, let it go! You want God to move...Let it go, so that he can move!

That girl you thought meant you some good is not your friend... Let her go! Honey, you know that man is not your husband....Let him go! Man, you know that surrounding you are in is not where you need to be...Let it go! Sweetheart, she's just not that into you...Let her go! No matter what you do for her, her feelings are not going to change. Let her go! You have given your all to him and he still doesn't want to marry you. Let him go! Even through his infidelity you have tried to make it work but he still wants Jill...Let him go, so that Jill can deal with the heartache and sleepless nights because the same thing he's doing to you, he'll do it to her too. Working two twelve hour shifts isn't going to make her satisfied because she constantly wants more. Let her go! Parents if you know you have raised up your children the right way and taught them right from wrong but they still want to do wrong, lovingly let them go! When they get of age you can't make them do what you want them to do, because you know when you thought you was grown couldn't nobody tell you what to do.

Let them live their lives, just like you're living yours. They are going to make mistakes, so let them make them. If you know your child is prone to getting in trouble and constantly going to jail or prison then obviously that's what they like, if not they would not keep getting in trouble to go to jail or prison. I'm teaching my child now and I told her now if you do anything bad enough for you to go to jail then yes, the first time you call me I'll get you out because that would be a learning experience for you. Now the second time you're going to have to sit there for a while until I feel like picking you up. Now after the third time you're on your own. I'm going to tell that officer to keep you in there and don't let you out until I get ready for you to be out. That's what I told my daughter. You can't keep encouraging and entertaining your child's idiocy. You see it as a way of love and support but they see it as a way to do things knowing that there will be somebody out there to get them up out of their mess.

There comes a time that you have to let your children know that you're not always going to be there when they do something wrong. You have got to train your children on how to handle trials and in life trials will come, but teaching them will prepare them and that preparation will enable them to follow the proper steps in handling those trials. They got to care enough about themselves to want to stay out of places like that. If you know you've done all you can for someone and they still aren't satisfied then let it go. If you know that he/she left another to be with you and then decided to do the same to you, well you should have left that back where you got it from. If you know you have everything your hearts desire (money, material things and a "good" woman/ man) but is still missing something else then set that all aside and get on your knees and find your missing piece. If you can't find peace in your own home, then you know you need to do some spring cleaning. Clean out every room from your attic to your basement because in each room it could hold some mess that you've been holding on to for a long time.

If you've had enough of you and is tired of driving yourself then humble yourself, give yourself over to God, let yourself go, so that God can be the One to take you up. Die to the old you, so that God can birth in you someone new. Set yourself free from all that you have allowed to hinder you. I know this is a bit off subject but I have to say this. I'm so tired of hearing black people say, "If it wasn't for the white folks or if it wasn't for those foreigners coming in and taking up all the... we would be fine." Black people I want you to understand something, it's not the white folks that are hindering you from making it in life, it's you. I know... I know... It's hard for you to believe but soak in that fact and digest it. Just like they had free education from grades K-12 so did you. They have to pay for college just like you do. It isn't their fault that their parents help prepare them for college so they won't have to pay. Not all white folks go to college off their parents, there are some who have to work hard for their education too and have to get financial aid. Not every white person in the world is rich, the one's who went out and made a difference for themselves are.

Whether their parents left it for them when they died or not, somebody still had to work hard to get it. You have the power to control your life, your finances and everything else, not the white man. Yes, back in time, the white man did take the black man into slavery and forced them to work. This is a new day and age and things have changed. I wasn't born into slavery, I wasn't a slave and I don't call nobody "Massa" and I am nobody's "nigger." I wasn't a slave to them and they can't and will not make me do anything I don't want to do. I wasn't brought to America on a boat from Africa. I was born in Georgia to a woman named Kawanda and I came out her... (you know what). I'm old enough to make my own decisions and choose my own path. That's another problem I have with black folks, why in the world is it okay to call each other a nigga? You don't hear white folks walking around calling each other a "cracker". Let me help you educate yourself a little bit. Learn to learn.

I can never understand why blacks and whites are still holding on to the past history that they had no affiliation with. Who told you that your ancestors were slaves? Who told you that your great, great, great, great grandfather was a slave owner? Someone had to educate you on this. Yes, those who had to endure slavery have a right to feel angry but why do you, if you've never experienced it? Those slaves have been dead for ages and so is their "Massa's". I understand that it is important to know about your history and I know it angers some of us to know how blacks were treated back then. But that doesn't make it right to hold that against every white person you meet. Yes I do believe there is racism in this world and I do believe there were courageous people like Harriet Tubman, Martin Luther King, Rosa Parks and others who paved the way for the freedom of blacks, but there was thousands of white folks who helped transport escaped slaves. Many may not believe this but there are some blacks who are just as racists as some whites probably even more. I personally don't have anything against the whites, one helped raised me. As a matter of fact Helen Beaty was a breath of fresh air for me. She took me into her home and treated me like I was her own. Color didn't matter. All that matter was the love we had for each other. She was another angel God sent to me and I'm thankful to have such an amazing woman in my life. She is the prime example of what love is. Do you really want to know why white folks got it all, it's because the blacks are too busy fighting against one another instead of pulling together and making a difference. The white folks came together, formulated a plan and went to go get what they wanted. Whether it's the jobs in America or the blacks from Africa. You're fighting against the wrong ethnic group. You're too busy fighting each other instead of coming together and doing something positive and effective for one another. I have never seen a group of people so jealous of one another, so envious and devious of what the other person got then the black community. I'm not saying that white folks will not rob or kill one another, but I am saying that it is so common in the black community for them to steal, kill and destroy one another then any other ethnic group in the world. That is sad. Black people you have got to stop hating each other and learn how to come together in love. You will hardly ever see white folks killing each other because the other person asks them for a cup of sugar.

White folks stick together, they make things happen for them and they go out there in do what ever need to be done at whatever risk. Blacks are too scared to take risk. They are afraid of losing the little that they have. Most of these white folks invest. They save and they flip their profits to make more. Don't get mad at the Indians and Chinese's for coming to America and creating their own businesses. You could have done the same if you had sense enough to educate yourself or follow your dreams. Most of the black folks I know can cook their behinds off, but most of them don't own their own restaurant. Most of my family can do hair real good but they refuse to open up their own beauty shop. Folks, take a stand, speak out, and don't hold back. Do what you got to do. If you want a business do what it takes to get that business. Stop blaming the white folks when you helped the white folks get to where they needed to be.

You talk about them but you spend all your money in their stores helping to make them rich. Get your own business so somebody can help you too. I have nothing against any race; I love all people no matter where they come from. If a person does good by me then I'll do good by them. I can't hate someone that has never done anything to me. So blacks, if you want power don't give other races the opportunity to take all the power. Get you some. They have paved the way for themselves because they did what they had to do now you got to pave the way for you. Don't get mad at them, do what they do, better yet find ways to do it better.

Conquer Your Fear

"You gain strength, courage and confidence by every experience in which you really stop to look fear in the face. You are able to say to yourself, 'I have lived through this horror. I can take the next thing that comes along.' You must do the thing you think you cannot do." ~ Eleanor Roosevelt

Conquer Your Fear 6

I THOUGHT I could never love another guy the way I loved Jim until I met Terrell. My relationship with him was nothing compared to Jim's because Terrell actually came after me. I thought I was in love with Jim but the way Terrell had me feeling it was like none other, so that's when I realized that I was actually in love. It must have been infatuation with Jim, because the first time I kissed Terrell electricity ignited every nerve in my body. Have anyone ever made you feel like you were floating but you were still on solid ground? Terrell had me feeling like I was floating on top of a cloud. I had the butterflies, the giddies and the giggles. He was in a place where we couldn't physically be together, but we made it work to the best of our abilities. I got passed his current situation; I looked over his flaws and we both found ways of making each other happy.

We wrote each other daily, talked on the phone all the time and we shared a lot of our thoughts and dreams but when I went through a situation I pushed him away because I thought I was doing what was best for him, only to realize that I was only doing what was best for me at that time. I pushed him out of the way because of fear. Fear of loving and being loved. Fear that I would give it all I had and end up getting hurt again. Fear of what could stand in our future. Fear of making yet another wrong decision. Jim had such an affect on me that I questioned whether Terrell really loved me; whether he'd one day get tired of me and be with someone else. There was a point in time where I stopped writing him and years passed and I'd moved on with somebody else. While in that relationship I still held on to Terrell, not giving the man I was with a chance to love me and I didn't give myself a chance to love him back.

I got back in touch with Terrell and we started talking again but I didn't feel right talking to him while I was living with another man. I was at my happiest with Terrell and with him was where I truly wanted to be, but I was unfair to the one I was with and I wanted to give him a chance, even if it meant taken away my own happiness. Have you ever been in love and was in a situation where the best thing you can do was the hardest thing you ever done, but you knew you had to do it cause it was the right thing to do? I can still memorize the letter I wrote to him telling him. I remember the tears that rolled down my cheeks as I formulated the words in my mind. I remember how much pain shot threw my heart as I was letting my pen bleed on that piece of paper as I told him how much I loved him, but how I thought we should separate. Although it hurt so bad to let him go, I had so much going on in my life, crowding my space that there was no room for him.

I have been setting my happiness aside for others for a long time, so I did it again. I let Terrell go. Did I give up on true love? Maybe. I tend to think that everything happens for a reason, but I also believe I allowed fear to rob me of true happiness. Several years passed and just when I was beginning to feel comfortable with who I was with, Terrell shows back up and caused my whole train of thought to shift. My emotions was all over the place but I also had a feeling that him coming back into my life was for a reason and I just had to be careful not to confuse those reasoning with something else. As we begin to talk, we dug a little deeper. He talked about how he felt when I broke it off with him. I tried to get him to understand why I did what I had to do. He objected and thought that if our love was strong enough then we could have stood the test of time.

I agreed but at the same time I tried to get him to understand I did what I did out of love. I didn't want my situation to affect him and it would have because I wouldn't have been able to be of service to him. Then he told me how he'd found love in someone else and how happy he was. It was painful listening to him say how she completed him because at one time I thought we'd completed each other. I must admit that I was at a state of confusion. My mind and my heart were going against one another.

"A heart ain't a brain but I think that I still love you. A happy

endin' makes it right. 'Cause it ends when you don't want to and it makes perfect sense to end it like the start but how do I explain this nonsense to my heart?" ~ *Chris Brown*

Was I confusing my bruised ego with love or was I hoping for something else? I didn't know but what I did know was that I did not like what I was hearing. I wanted to be happy for him but what I was feeling was conflicting with my senses. I mean what did I expect? Did I really believe he'd wait for me? Was I expecting him too? I couldn't be mad at the decision he made and as the days passed my common sense begin to kick in. As I begin to talk to him more, I realized how much he'd changed into a person that I didn't recognize. Then I realized that I was in love with who he once was and what we had before but those days was long gone and so was my lost love. The person that he showed me from way back when and that man that I loved so much was no longer there. For so long I was unable to really move on because I held on to him, wondering what he was doing; what it would have been like if we wouldn't have never broken up; and what it would be like if I ever talked to him again.

At the time when he broke the news to me about his present girlfriend I didn't want to hear it, I was crushed and I begin to realize how he felt when I chose someone else over him. I was now on the receiving end. Apart of me wished that I'd never met him and another part of me was happy that he showed me who he really was and how he really felt. I knew that I needed him to tell me so that I could replace the broken piece that was misplaced from way back when. I realized that he was apart of my past and in my future I had someone else who wanted to love me and had done all he can to do so. I realized that I had to go through this step to be able to set myself free and set him free as well. I was in the healing process. I know longer wondered what it would be like if we talked again. I knew we were now in two different worlds, with two different mindsets and with two different hearts.

I thought we were one, and if we'd listen close enough we'd hear that our hearts had the same rhythm. I thought he was my soul mate, the one that I would have more kids with and the one that I would spend the rest of my life with. I'd dreamt about it and even fantasized about it but that's all it had been dreams and fantasies. Him coming back into my life was a way for us both to get the closure that we needed. He needed to know why I left and I needed to know if the feelings I felt for him was still there. A heavy weight was lifted off of me and I was no longer running, no longer wondering and I realized that I will no longer hinder myself from love out of fear again. My fear was losing him and I ran away to avoid that and he ran into the arms of another woman that obviously could love him better. In time I found a man that can love me best. I will always have respect, love and appreciation for Terrell, because whether he knows it or not, he helped me conquer my fears.

He taught me to stand up for what I believe in and not always run from what I can't see. I promised my self that this come around, in my future relationship, I'm going to love and I'm going to finally let my heart be the director. I have not only feared love but I've feared making mistakes. I've made so many careless mistakes in my life to the point that I was willing to stay in one situation out of fear that I would be making yet another mistake. I was afraid of going towards my goals and dreams out of fear that things wouldn't go the way I wanted them to go. I had fear of not having enough. Fear of failure. I'd had doubt in my abilities and at one time I was even afraid to serve God out of fear that the devil would come after me, but when I discovered my true identity I realized that I could not live my life in fear because if I allowed fear to continue to take control of my life, then my life would have been wasted. Then I came to realization that the things I feared the most had already happened to me.

To dream anything that you want to dream. That is the beauty of the human mind. To do anything that you want to do. That is the strength of the human will. To trust yourself to test your limits. That is the courage to succeed. ~ Bernard Edmonds

In the Word, we are often encouraged to never fear. God does not install in any of us the Spirit of fear. Satan has no problem with putting fear in us, to keep us in bondage. He will put thoughts into your head that does not make sense to you. He will try to paralyze and try to cripple you with that thing called "fear". But I have declared that I am taking everything back what the devil stole from me. The self-esteem I'd lost, all the happiness that was snatched away from me, all the courage, the passion, the goals and the dreams that I once had, everything... Who said I couldn't do it this way because if I did it would be another way? Who in the world said I couldn't make it work? Who said I can't get another job because of my past history? Who said I couldn't make my dreams come true? I want to know who said I couldn't walk towards my destiny. Who said I wasn't purposed? Who said I wasn't good enough or wise enough? Who said I wasn't skinny enough? Who said I wasn't strong enough? Who said it?

There is a time when you have to act like fear doesn't even exist. Become ignorant to it. Don't give yourself time to think about it because when you begin to think on it feelings begin to set in. Instead of being committed to fear and doubt, commit yourself and your time in having faith in yourself and believe in all the things you can do. You have to stand up and have the courage to live; the courage to stare fear in the face and tell it what to do and what you're going to do. Life and death are in the power of the tongue. God created the world alone by speaking. Just like he spoke life into the world, you too can speak life into you. Always think, consider, act, proceed and verbalize positivity in your life. Be content in who you are and what you believe in. No matter what people think about you, think good thoughts about yourself. By me knowing who I am, can't nothing or nobody tell me what I am not. I am who God says I am! In order to be victorious you have to take action.

Action disperses fear and if you sit still long enough fear will try to creep in, so move forward towards your goals and be diligent, have faith and always trust in God. "For I am the Lord, your God, who takes hold of your right hand and says to you, Do not fear; I will help you (Isaiah 41:13)." Allow him to help you get passed your doubts and allow Him to hold your hand when you feel helpless. There is nothing that God is unable to do. He is the source of everything and in everything anything is possible for those who love the Lord. His Word says, "That I am more than a conqueror and I can do all things through Christ who strengthens me." Without Him, I would not have any victory over sin. Without Him, we would all fall victim to the wrath to come. Without Jesus we can do nothing and we have no hope in this world without God. Just stand firm and don't allow the devil to win. The devil is defeated every time you fail to listen to him. The devil can't take anything from you unless you give him room to take it. I encourage you to take back what the devil stole from you. It doesn't belong to him. Take it all back, it's yours.

Living Authentically For God

"I have been crucified with Christ; nevertheless, I live; yet not I, but Christ liveth in me." ~ Galatians 2:20

Living Authentically For God 7

AS I SAID before, I've always had a desire to be closer to God. Every being in my body has been triggered to love Him. Not because someone told me that I must do it, but when I *thought* about all of the things that the Lord has done for me, I begin to *feel* affection for Him so strongly that I begin to genuinely *love* Him. When I got tired of thinking for myself and making decisions for myself, which resulted to me backsliding so many times with no sound results, I made up in my mind that I would let the Lord do what He needed to do when it came to me. So, I asked myself... self... myself said, huh... I said self, "How can I be of service to God? How can I prove to Him that I am grateful for what He's done and shower Him with the love I have for Him? I know that there is nothing I can do to repay Him for what He's done, so what can I do to be pleasing unto Him." I started reading the Word, not sure at the time as to what I was reading. I flipped through the Bible and stayed in book of Romans.

I read all of Romans but chapter 12 verses one stuck with me, it said, "I beseech, you therefore, brethren, by the mercies of God, that you present your bodies as a living sacrifice, holy and acceptable to God, which is your reasonable service." So I asked myself, what does that mean? Myself responded, "Just as it says, we can never fully repay Him for all that He has done but be consistently honest and sacrificial to God. Give yourself away to Him, therefore, your body no longer belongs to you (as you once thought) but it is now handed over to

God. Constantly seek His face, constantly worship and give Him all the praise. Follow His commands, do what He has already told you to do. Be obedient, love others and really and truly believe in Him and what He can do. Open up yourself completely to Him so that you can useable for Him." So then I asked myself, "How will I be able to know what God can use me for, where He can use me at and when is a good time for me to be useable?" Myself responded, "live authentically for God."

Living authentically for you is one thing, but living authentically for God is a whole other way of living. I looked up authentic and it means not false or copied, genuine and real.When you begin living an authentic life, you are living the life that resonates with your inner being. Your authentic, divine self was made in the image of God. If you can begin to identify with the love and intention with which God formed you perhaps grasp the magnificence and majesty of your being and fully embrace the power and beauty with which you were created, you may be able to shake free from all those little things that is tying you down. You will not bind yourself with caustic and destructive *habits*, relationships or lifestyles. You will gain inner strength and let go of manipulation, power plays, cruelty and hatred. You will find that your life is being elevated to a higher spiritual level. You will be thinking of humankind, rather than self. You won't be afraid of truth, and will deal with fear in a better way.

The Bible says, "When Christ who is our life appears, then you also will appear with Him in glory. Therefore put to death your members which are on the earth: fornication, uncleanness, passion, evil desire, and covetousness, which is idolatry. But now you yourselves are to put off all these: anger, wrath, malice, blasphemy, filthy language out your mouth. Do not lie to one another, since you have put off the old man with his deeds, and have put on the new man who is renewed in knowledge according to the image of Him who created him (Colossians 3:4-10). You will no longer be concerned or sucked into the things of this world. You will set your mind on things above, not on things on this earth. To live authentically for God is to check your heart, learn to surrender, die to live, spiritually feed yourself, have faith, pray without ceasing and behave like a Christian.

CHECK YOUR HEART

This takes me to the story in1 Samuel 16:6-7, when Samuel saw Eliab and thought, "Surely the Lord's anointed stands here before the Lord. But the Lord said to Samuel, "Do not consider his appearance or his height, for I have rejected him. The Lord does not look at the things man looks at. Man looks at the outward appearance, but the Lord looks at the heart." I hear folk always saying, "God knows my heart." Indeed He does. As a matter of fact for the righteous He test the hearts and minds. So, you have to be careful what you allow to flow in your mind and also be careful of what you are carrying around in your heart. Take an inventory of what you are carrying with you and ask God to remove anything from your heart that will distract you from living in truth and authentically. Make sure your heart does not carry any secret goals any deflected motivations. God wants us to have a pure and genuine heart; the kind of heart that keeps your motivations, goals, words, thoughts and actions in sync. Be reminiscent, reminding yourself to intensely dissect yourself. Examine your intentions so your outward excellence will not be compromised by inward distractions or crooked secrets.

SURRENDER

From the beginning of time God had given man the choice to surrender to Him. Adam and Eve were given the choice when He said, "you shall not" instead of "you cannot". From the beginning He has given us the ability to choose. Either Adam or Eve will obey Him and live or they will give into the momentary desires of their hearts and die. I know that the devil tricked them but they did have a choice. Had they made the choice of surrendering the longings of their hearts to God, it is a possibility that we all may be living eternally within a perfect world, but since the devil felt like entertaining and because of their disobedience, our hearts have become more prone to selfishness with each generation. Think about Cain and Abel now think about the people in this world who are killing one another. But we can't blame Adam and Eve for everything. Just like God had given them the choice to surrender, He also gives us that same choice. They were just the first ones to fail.

Surrender means to yield ownership, to relinquish control over what we consider ours: our property, our time, and our "rights." Surrendering to God means that we are acknowledging the fact that we are not our own, but we belong to God. What we have and what we think we own actually belongs to God. After all it is because of God that we have what we have. He is the giver of all good things. We admit that He is in control of everything— our circumstances and situations. By surrendering we are putting away the things that is hindering us and holding us back from what God has for us. Everything that is keeping you from reaching your fullest potential must go. Put it all away in a box and hand it over to Him. We let go of whatever it is that's keeping us from wanting God's ways. You have to give all of you away, holding nothing back so that the Lord can use you. You humbly allow Him to work in you, taking out all that trash that you have cluttered into your space. He has to download and upload; tear down some stuff and rebuild; cleanse and purify; break some yokes and set free.

DIE TO LIVE

When we surrender and put all of our trust in God, we are incorporated into, united to, Jesus, which includes being united to His death. Jesus death becomes our death. So we must die to sin and become alive in God. Romans 6: 6-14 better explains it, "Knowing this, that our old man is crucified with him, that the body of sin might be destroyed, that henceforth we should not serve sin. For he that is dead is freed from sin. Now if we be dead with Christ, we believe that we shall also live with him: Knowing that Christ being raised from the dead dieth no more; death hath no more dominion over him. For in that he died, he died unto sin once: but in that he liveth, he liveth unto God. Likewise reckon ye also yourselves to be dead indeed unto sin, but alive unto God through Jesus Christ our Lord. Let not sin therefore reign in your mortal body, that ye should obey it in the lusts thereof. Neither yield ye your members as instruments of unrighteousness unto sin: but yield yourselves unto God, as those that are alive from the dead, and your members as instruments of righteousness unto God. For sin shall not have dominion over you: for ye are not under the law, but under grace. Transform from being a slave to sin to slaves of God." We are all slaves to something at least you can benefit from being a slave to God. Again, the Word can explain it better. "Do you not know that to who you present yourselves slaves to obey, you are that one's slaves whom you obey, whether of sin leading to death, or of obedience leading to righteousness? For when you were slaves of sin, you were free in regard to righteousness." What fruit did you have then in the things of which you are now ashamed? For the end of those things is death. "But now having being set free from sin, and having become slaves of God, you have your fruit to holiness, and the end, everlasting life. For the wages of sin is death but the gift of God is eternal life (Romans 6:16-23)."

SPIRITUAL FOOD

Many of you are malnourished and lack spiritual food. Some of you may not even know who Adam and Eve is. To feed ourselves, we must first purge ourselves. If a man therefore purge himself from these, he shall be a vessel unto honour, sanctified, and meet for the master's use, and prepared unto every good work (2Timothy 2:21). The Bible is a guide to how to live daily for God. Spiritually feed yourself, do not always depend on the pastor to feed it to you. If you don't understand ask God to give you understanding of His Word and He will. By His Word we become strong in the Lord and reach a level of maturity in Him. Become obese in the Word of God. Eat so much of it until you can't eat no more and when the food from which you ate digest get you some more. The Word of God is essential when it comes to living accordingly to God. In the beginning was the Word, and the Word was with God, and the Word was God.

"All Scripture is given by inspiration of God, and is profitable for doctrine, for reproof, for correction, for instruction in righteousness, that the man of God may be complete, thoroughly equipped for every good work (2 Timothy 3:16-17)." I said this to remind you how important the Word of God is. To know God is to know His Word; to know what He did and to know how to live in order to make it into the Kingdom. I know many feel like the Bible is man made and it cannot be trusted. For those of you who feel this way, here is what I suggest you do. Get on your knees pray to God and ask Him if the Word from the Bible is true and if not then ask Him to introduce Himself to you. Get to know more about Him then what man say. Get to know Him for yourself. If you listen long enough and be sincere in your prayer He'll answer you. Allow Him to pour into you the Holy Spirit, which will speak into you. Get drunk off of the Holy Spirit of God. In my opinion, the Bible in which we read today doesn't teach anything wrong but teaches us how to love and be better people, so if anyone finds anything wrong in that, then take that up with God.

THE POWER OF: PRAYER, FASTING, FAITH PRAISE & WORSHIP

Pray without ceasing. Be consistent in prayer. Meditate on the Lord. Prayer changes things and gives you strength. It's like a blanket that warms you when you're cold. It gives you rest when you're under distress. It gets you out of a situation when you're in trouble. It guards you; keep you safe when you feel endangered. It's your shelter in the times of storms. And when you pray, believe that God can do exactly what He said He would do. Have faith in God and have faith in yourself and your abilities. God installs in each of us a measure of faith. The Bible says, we can move mountains with faith as small as a mustard seed. Don't spend hours and hours on the floor crying and slobbering just to get up and allow the devil to put unbelief in you. You just wasted 6 hours. I don't think it takes hours and hours to get a break through.

The Lord even agrees with me in Matthew 6:7-8 saying, "And when you pray, do not keep on babbling like pagans, for they think they will be heard because of their many words. Do not be like them, for your Father knows what you need before you ask Him." Why exhaust God? You don't have to say it over and over again, He heard what you said when you said it the week before. If you trust in God with all your heart without any hint of doubt then He would move. I love praying to God and the best church service I ever been to is the church service I have in my room between me and God. I don't have to prove anything to anyone. I don't have to wait until church service to pray and have church. I loved when Jesus spoke to the people about prayer. He told them when praying; do not be like the hypocrites, for they love to pray standing in the synagogues and on the street corners to be seen by men.

But when you pray, go into your room, close the door and pray to your Father, who is unseen. Then your Father, who sees what is done in secret, will reward you. I'm not saying it's not okay to pray in church and around people but it depends on your intentions. Are you praying to get a breakthrough or for show? It is a good thing to get behind the veil of God in your secret place and pour your heart and soul out to God. The best artistic and authentic thing that I ever learned to master is the art of praise and worship. Understand that praise and worship is definitely necessary, it's beneficial and advantageous. God is moved when we worship and praise Him. Things happen when you get behind the veil with Him and meditate on His goodness. Instead of worrying about a situation that I can't solve I just give it all over to God and praise Him. I praise my way through a situation. I worship my way through the struggles I face throughout the day.

I praise Him when I'm feeling good and when I'm feeling bad. When things are going well and when things are not going too well. I praise Him when I'm broke and I praise Him when that check clears. I praise Him even though I may not have everything that I want but because I have everything I need I give Him all the praise. There are times when I just praise Him just because He's who He is. When I think about His goodness, my heart is filled with love and I can't help but worship Him. When I think about what He brought me out of and where I am today I praise Him. When I think about His Son dying on the cross for little ol' me, yes I worship Him. When I think about how many times He'd forgiven me I praise Him so much that I get exhausted. There are times when I think about how the seasons change and how each and everything serves a purpose here on Earth and I thank Him for giving us the knowledge to understand the circle of life.

I have the tendency of singing to him songs that I create on my own so that He could hear the sweet sound of my heart-felt words. After all He has done I have a right to praise Him! I wouldn't mind shouting to the hills to tell anyone how good my God is. So don't be ashamed or limit yourself on prayer, praise and worship because God recognizes that as an honor unto Him and if you honor Him He will show His appreciation.

BE OF SERVICE TO SOMEONE ELSE

I'm still trying to wrap my mind around some save folk who feel that they are too holy to associate with the unsaved. You can talk the talk but fail to walk the walk, you stumbling. Even Jesus made Himself available for those who didn't believe in Him. Why? Because He didn't come into the world to boast or flaunt around who He was. His job was to save souls and show people that there was hope in the near future. He didn't have to brag about who He was because His actions spoke for Him. When He spoke and when He made an entrance, He didn't have to prove Himself because the way He carried Himself said it all. He spoke with authority, hope, love, power and in peace. If He can let down his guard and get on a level where He can save someone else life then so can you. Surely, you're not better than He who gives life.

You are not too save that you can't speak life into somebody else. You never know how much that person testimony can be a blessing to you. You must have forgotten that at one time somebody had to pray for you. There was many times than one that Jesus has interceded for you. Oh how quickly one forgets how many times their mothers, fathers, preachers and anybody else who loved them had to get on their knees and tears, praying that God protect them and forgive them through their mess. Then there are some save folks who act like they haven't never heard a curse word in all their lives, knowing when they was in their mess they said and probably knew more curse words then that person, could say some things that'll make a sailor blush and if somebody say something they don't like, they will put down their holy cards and tell you about yourself and probably be ready to fight. Now you know at one point you too had given all of you to someone that didn't mean you any good.

It was not long before God delivered you from your addictions. At one point nobody could keep you from smoking your cigarettes before, after and between meals. Your day would have not been the same without you taking a sip of your beer, wine or vodka. Or did you forget that God sent someone your way to help you deal with your depression and cry for help. Did you forget about the many times that you were in clubs and bars right along with the same one's you're condemning, maybe even more then they was. You knew you were fornicating, committing adultery and prostituting your body, abusing your temple (which is your body) making it available to anyone who had a quick dollar or who you felt that could love you more. Lest you quickly forget how somebody had to help you when you didn't have a place to lay your head or didn't have any food to eat. Or let's talk about the time you got arrested and wanted somebody to write you a letter, put money on your books and give you a place to parole out at when you came home. You were in them same streets, doing some or all of the same things and singing the same tunes. But you must have forgotten. Let he who is without sin cast the first stone.

Don't worry I'll wait...

Nobody is perfect and we all fall short. Even save folks make mistakes, but even through the mistakes God never gave up on you. To be like Jesus you have to be able to get into the dirt to get to the treasure. You have not always been clean. You carried so much dirt at one time that nobody but the Lord could do the cleaning for you. Be of help to someone, take somebody by the hand and help lead them. Give someone a shoulder to cry on, a hand to reach out to and the patience it takes to help them go through what they have to go through. Show them the true love of God that flows through you. Accept one another, then, just as Christ accepted you, in order to bring praise to God (Romans 15:7). Therefore as the elect of God, holy and beloved, put on tender mercies, kindness, humility, meekness, long suffering; bearing with one another and forgiving one another, but above all these thing put on love, which is the bond of perfection and let the peace of God rule in your hearts (Colossians 3:12-14).

Get a relationship with God and He will put in you the Holy Spirit, which is apart of Him, and He will be able to speak through the Spirit what is needed of you. But you have to be able to first humble yourself in order to allow God to speak. You must ask God to help you differentiate your ways of thinking into His ways. You must learn how to set apart what He speaks into you, what the devil speaks to you and what you're speaking into yourself. Ask Him to help you get a clear ear to hear His voice, so that you can know when He speaks to you. We all have a race to run and a path that we must walk on. Often times we decrease in speed during the race and at times we may walk in the wrong path. There is a God who don't mind giving us the energy to run faster and don't mind guiding us in the right direction.

There is nothing wrong with making mistakes and sometimes we have to go through some mess. There's no testimony unless you go through the test and you want get the message if you don't go through the mess. When you're going through the test and waddling in your mess, just praise God in advance. Ask Him, what is it is that you must learn through all of it and how can you use it towards your purpose. And in finding your purpose or after God help you get to your purpose, as I said be of service to somebody else. I encourage you to leave everything behind that does not belong to your divine, authentic, God-made self.

Not an Ordinary Love

"For God so loved the world that He gave His only begotten Son…"
~ John 3:16

Not an Ordinary Love

8

GOD'S LOVE FOR US is immeasurable beyond competition and above all else selfless. From the beginning of creation, He knew all along that Lucifer would deceive Him, He knew from the moment He made Adam into dust and took a rib to create Eve that the devil would con Eve and that He would have to come down in the image of a man revealed to be the Son of Man to die for the sins of the world. All along He knew and He'd never tried to deny us of freewill. He knew that we would disobey Him, deny Him and above all else kill His Son but He still saw fit for us to live. His love never changes...He never changes...He has always been the same God...Never changing.

It took an extraordinary love to love me. It took someone patient enough to deal with my ways; someone faultless enough to look beyond my faults. Someone wise enough to know that I'm not perfect and I will make mistakes. Someone understanding enough to understand why I'm the way that I am and in that understanding look into my heart and do what needs to be done to shower their love into a heart that was hardened. Mend a heart that had many broken pieces. Give comfort to a heart that was in pain. Put love into a heart that was loveless. Give peace to a mind that was disordered. Dig deep inside of a person that was dirty and do a supernatural cleansing with hyssop and with water that is purer then any water man have ever tasted.

That type of love that corrects when you make an error. That GPS when you've lost your way. When everyone you thought loved you turn against you,

He's there to remind you that His love never changes, no matter what the season is. When your wife, husband, boyfriend, girlfriend or lover use you, hurt you and break your heart there is a man that I know who can come in and wash all that pain away. He can dry your tears and hold you late in the midnight hour and if you give it all to Him, He will turn your situation around. He still loves you, even in your wrongdoing. He hurts when you hurt; He knows when you can't even comprehend and when you feel like you can't take no more, He is there to remind us that we are stronger than what meets the eye. When we feel we can't make it to the top of the mountain, He is there to remind us that we only have a few more climbs to go.

When you don't have any more strength, He is your strength. When a battle is too much for you, He fights it for you. I don't know about you but I need that very special kind of love; the kind of love that remains the same no matter what. There's nothing like it and there is nothing like the love of God. I don't need that ordinary love that the world likes to give. They can keep that love that changes. One day you love me the next day you can't stand me. One day you can't live without me the next day you don't need me. One day I'm your best friend the next day you stabbing me in the back. One day I have all that you need but when it's gone you don't come around any more.

Do you know what love is? Ask yourself what it is and then look in the Bible and see if you can put a check mark on every word that explains what love really is? In 1 Corinthians 13:4 it speaks on love saying, "Love is patient, love is kind. It does not envy, it does not boast, it is not proud. It is not rude, it is not self-seeking, it is not easily angered, and it keeps no record of wrongs. Love does not delight in evil but rejoices with the truth. It always protects, always trusts, always hopes, and always perseveres. Love never fails." So, where you able to check all of these key factors of love? How many of us can say we have mastered the true meaning of love? It's not that ordinary love that man tends to give it's that real love. Real love is unquenchable. Song of Solomon (8:7) says, "Many waters cannot quench love, neither can the floods drown it."

Real love knows no boundaries and does not have a scale weighing how much love to put into something. Real love is sacrificial. Sacrificial love is to love unselfishly and to be self-sacrificial with sincere motivations to help others in their sufferings; always seeing the good in others, regardless of their flaws and without judgment. To love without motive. Loving so much that regardless of the cost you're willing to do all you can for the help of others. Jesus Christ offered His life to redeem us from sin and Moses risked his life for the sake of his people. Paul the apostle used the word agape to define unselfish love, it is something you do. To love is to be *committed*. Jesus gave a command that we ought to love one another as He has loved us. He added that and if you have love for one another, then everyone will know that you are my disciples (John 13:34-35). Love is not an option.

He gave a command that was not up for suggestions or recommendations. If He knew it was unfeasible to love like He loved then He wouldn't have never command that we do so. As humans we just have a way of rebelling against the idea of pure unconditional love. Many believe that such love is impossible somehow out of place in this world. We love others to a certain degree. We'll love based on how others act towards us. There is a line that we have drawn when it comes to loving. We believe that there is only so much love that we are capable or prepared to give to another, that as far as you've already gone to do something kind for someone is the farthest as you can go. You believe that the people you already love are the only ones that you are prepared to love. We are content and okay with loving selectively. We are most comfortable with the kind of love that doesn't make us uncomfortable. *"As I have loved you, so you must love one another."*

You think when Jesus died on a cross He did it for a selective few? You think He drew a line? Not at all, His love was limitless. He loved us sacrificially by giving Himself away. He didn't think about how painful it would be to be whipped, flogged and nailed to a cross. He looked beyond that pain and felt that all He had to endure was worth it for His people. He gives honest, sincere, genuine and compassionate love. We find it hard to love like Jesus commanded because it goes against how we were taught and against our humanly nature. It's against reasoning and logic. It is difficult to practice something that has never been taught the right way. As a child we were taught to love who loved us; to dislike who disliked us; to have hatred towards those who did wrong against us or against the one's we love. We were taught that love was proven through what a person gives. If he/she gives me attention then they like me or love me.

Oh, you bought me a diamond ring and a lot of expensive materialistic things then he/she must really love and care about me. We're living in the world of selfishness, hate and deceit. We look passed those who are in need and have been conditioned to make up excuses why we should study to mind our own business when getting involved in other people's lives. It's so easy to be selfish, ignore someone who needs love, support and guidance. It would seem as if loving like Jesus has loved us is humanly unattainable. I know there are some people who sometimes practice love on certain occasions but loving others sacrificially and unconditionally all the time is a bit much. Many people can't even meet loves expectations. Not because it is impossible to do so but many will not humble themselves to the challenge of actually loving. When we have a relationship with Jesus our ability to love comes easy. When we become Children of God and allow Him to take over our perspectives are different.

Jesus said "when you give yourself to me I am apart of you and walk in my ways." So if we are walking in His ways and are truly apart of Him then it will be possible that we can love. You love by being of service to someone else and not always thinking about yourself. You love when you sit down with someone, listen to their problems and give advice, you love when you pray for someone else instead of yourself all the time. You love when you give without wanting anything back. Love is patient, love is kind... and yes although we are not perfect it does not mean we can't love like we ought too. We make mistakes but just as Paul made a mistake and denied Jesus three times, he had the decency to recognize that he was wrong, wept and ask for forgiveness and God loved him all the same. He accepted him, even when he was flawed. That's love. When you're able to accept someone even though they are not perfect then that's perfect love. Not just love to your friends and family but to the people you don't even know including your enemies.

When you get to a level of maturity in God and His love flows through you then you're able to forgive and let go of stuff that can't get you to where you need to be. You no longer hold on to things like that because you realize that kindness kills all strife and if the person still got a problem pray for them with love and keep it moving. No it's not impossible to love like Jesus love if you apply love to each and every individual each day. We are to all bear each other burdens. The bible insist that we "those who are strong ought to bear with the failings of the weak and not please ourselves. Each of us should please his neighbour for his good, to build him up. For even Christ did not please himself, but, as it is written: "The insults of those who insult you have fallen on me (Romans 15:1-3)."

As a matter of fact before we start to pray we are told that if we have anything against another we are to correct it. I'm recognizable to the fact that we are human and that we have a flesh that must be crucified daily. We have an adversary in the devil who seeks only to destroy us and see us fail. Then to add on to that we have people to deal with in this world; all of this combined make our lives difficult. Jesus did say that we would have tribulation and that sometimes includes getting hurt by the people we love. I understand that everybody is not going to love you, everybody is not going to care about you, and people are going to misuse you, abuse you and maybe even hate you. Yet and still forgiving is what we should do. How many times we are to forgive, 7 times? No, Jesus said 7 times 70! Even at the cross Jesus prayed for those who hated him, saying "Father, forgive them, for they know not what they do (Luke 23:34)." After all that they had done to Him He still practiced His love. I'm sure we all have our pride but we must realize that pride in itself is also a sin. Learn how to care enough about someone else just like God cared enough about you. If we can feel His love, then we will know how to apply it to others.

Growing in Wisdom

"Wisdom is knowing what to do next; skills is knowing how to do it and virtue is doing it..." ~ David Starr Jordan

Growing in Wisdom

9

THE OLDER YOU get, the wiser you should become if you've learned lessons in life. There's no such thing as 40 being the new 20 and 60 being the new 40. If you're 40, you're 40 it isn't no subtracting. Everyday you live on this earth you're getting older. Don't be ashamed of getting old because there are some who don't live long enough to see adulthood. Appreciate the fact that God gave you a long life and is still giving it. It's crazy to me when I hear people saying how they wish they were younger and that they would like to stay a certain age forever. One day talk to an old man/woman who have lived their life, gone through their struggles and conquered them. They will amaze you! You have to be careful what you wish for or you might get it.

Let me give you an example, Barbara wanted to stay young forever, at the age of 35 she went through Botox to look younger and by the age of 45 she constantly said, "I don't want to see 50" and guess what Barbara got what she wished for. At the age of 49 she died of a heart attack. Even though this is a made up story I said all this to say that you should be grateful for the years you have. I'm thankful for a new life. I cherish every moment of life that God has given me. I want to wake up every morning; I want every year, every birthday that the good Lord gives to me. And every year that He gives to me I want be better. We don't get older we get experienced if you are wiser. If I live to see pass 50 I consider myself blessed and I'll be very happy too because I can get a senior citizen discount on a lot of stuff and I will have an excuse to park in the handicap space at every store. Not only that I would have the opportunity to see my child grow up and become a woman.

With the high prices we battle with today any discount will do. That's a blessing when you live pass other folks. What's that saying, "Old fools were once young fools?"I think that is for those people who did not learn in their younger years and brought the same mess in their adulthood. There are still old fools walking around. There's nothing like them. I have come across people who are 30 and 60 years old but still act as foolish as they did when they were 15 and 21; thirty-five still living at home with your mama. Get up, get out and get a life.

❧❈❧

There are many people who wish to be wise, yet they have the wrong concepts of what wisdom really is. One would think being wise is being a genius. Having a vast amount of knowledge does not make you wise it just makes you educated. Many believe that understanding knowledge is being wise. Not exactly. One may ask, just what is wisdom? Is it different from knowledge and wisdom? Knowledge is defined as a collection of facts, information, and/or skills acquired through experience or education or the theoretical or practical understanding of a subject. So, everything that is learned in school, from the Bible and through other experiences throughout life is knowledge. Scholars and scientist spend most of their lives studying and doing research which is why they obtain much knowledge. Yet, without being correctly applied, knowledge is worthless.

According to the thesaurus understanding which is also called intellection, is a psychological process related to an abstract or physical object, such as a   person, situation, or message whereby one is able to think about it and use concepts to deal adequately with that object. Understanding is a relation between the knower and an object of understanding. Understanding implies abilities and dispositions with respect to an object of knowledge sufficient to support intelligent behavior. An understanding is the limit of a *conceptualization*. To understand something is to have conceptualized it to a given measure. Understanding is a significant facet that relates directly to knowledge and wisdom. To understand means to be a step above knowledge.

It is the ability to give evaluation to knowledge. To understand knowledge is to see the *meaning or significance* of the knowledge.

So what is WISDOM?

In defining wisdom it means to have a deep understanding and realization of people, things, events or situations, resulting in the ability to chose or act or inspire to consistently produce the optimum results with a minimum of time, energy or thought. It is the ability to optimally apply perceptions and knowledge and so produce the desired results. Through knowledge we learn to act in our own best interest. Yet, wisdom gives a reflection of the values and criteria that applies to our knowledge. Wisdom is not about knowing good and evil but is knowing good from evil.

The Essence of Wisdom

... is to have the serenity to accept the things we cannot change, the courage to change the things that we can, and the wisdom to know the difference. ~ *Adapted from the Serenity Prayer*

Just how vital is it to obtain WISDOM?

Proverbs 3: 14-15 says, "Blessed is the man that findeth wisdom, and is rich in prudence. The purchasing thereof is better than the merchandise of silver, and her fruit than the chief and purest gold. She is more precious than all riches: and all the things that are desired are not to be compared to her. To be wise is to be teachable, observant, willing and the willingness to mature. In the words of Peter Sinclair, "The over-riding and enduring evidence of someone who is wise are the foundations of integrity and humility that have been forged throughout the years within the fabric of their beings. The more they grow the less they realize they know. They are in no need of self promotion. They have no desire to raise themselves above others. They flow seamlessly between those surrounded by abundance and those surrounded by lack. They are at home in the solitude as they are in the noise of civilization. Slow to speak. Quick to listen. Ever observing. Attuned to good counsel. Commonsensical in all matters. Disciplined. Persistent. Blessed. Righteous. Just. Insightful. Virtuous. They have no company with that which is evil. Discrete. Knowledgeable. Lovers of truth. Far more wealthy than any money could ever purchase. They are honored with a name that is defined by goodness and by an abundance of life." It was so important that even Eve had a desire for it which contributed in her fall.

How do we obtain WISDOM?

"The fear of the Lord is the beginning of wisdom; a good understanding has all those who do His commandments (Psalms 111:10)." God is the source of wisdom. For the Lord gives wisdom; From His mouth come knowledge and understanding (*Proverbs 2:6*). Solomon takes the meaning of wisdom to a different level, saying that wisdom is above all knowledge of the goodness of God and of His power. "But thou, our God, art kind and true, patient, and ruling all things in mercy. To know thee is complete righteousness, and to know thy power is the root of immortality. (Proverbs 15:1-3). Wisdom dwells with God and one can only obtain it from Him. "For she is a breath of the power of God, and a pure emanation of the glory of the Almighty. She is a reflection of eternal light, a spotless mirror of the working of God, and an image of his goodness (Proverbs 7:25-26)."

One my favorite books in the Bible is the book of Proverbs. There's nothing like obtaining wisdom and knowledge that is encouraged by God. The book of Proverbs is known as the book of Wisdom, written by Solomon, who was the wisest of all men (excluding Jesus). He prayed for wisdom and God bestowed it upon him. This book is full of lessons encouraging the children of God to grow in wisdom, knowledge and understanding. It is like a guide to becoming mature.

Wisdom tends to grow in proportion to one's awareness of one's ignorance.' *~Anthony De Mello*

From an early age, we should of been taught on how to obtain wisdom, so that we would become teachable to our children.. Encourage your children, friends and siblings to grow in wisdom, which is the Word of God. Educate them and be an example to them, help them learn what it takes to run a home, to first be a man or a woman then how to become a wife and a husband and to be domestically inclined. To grow in maturity not based on what they say but what they do. Not by their words alone but in their actions and deeds. Help them to grow in understanding, knowing what to expect in the real world and how to be more responsible. Be honest with your kids don't try to keep everything from them. Allow them to be able to make decisions and make choices in their own lives without interference. Since a child we have been told how to feel and what we are not "old enough" to feel.

We have been scared to open up our mouths because too many times we have been slapped in it for speaking on how we feel. We have been conditioned not to express our emotions. Have you ever heard someone or have been told by someone as a child that you were too young to feel aggravated, tired, exhausted or angry? Children have feelings just like adults do. As a child I could remember getting a beating for whatever reason and told to shut my mouth while they were still hitting me. I mean what do they expect? If you keep hitting me I am going to feel the pain and my reaction to that pain is crying. Maybe if they would of stop hitting me the pain would have subsided and I would have stopped crying. Now the most ignorant thing I dislike is how some adults curse around their kids and then want to hit them when they repeat what is being said.

We are taught that cursing is wrong but yet we are surrounded around an environment and people that curse. Children are like sponges they mimic what they hear and do what they see others do. A child doesn't know anything unless they hear it. In hearing it they are learning it and in learning it they are being taught it and if they are taught it eventually they are going to say it. Why your child cursed or who they learned how to curse from? They heard it from somewhere maybe mommy, daddy, auntie, uncle, grandma, cousin, friends, etc. We can't protect our kids from cursing because reality is people do curse but we can teach them what not to say and not say it ourselves. We are taught not to be in grown folks business yet we are exposed to grown folks situations. We are told to keep our mouths shut because we told the truth about something that mommy didn't want everyone to know. What does that do to a child? It causes them to be silent when someone ask them a question and/or for the truth.

If mommy don't feel like talking on the phone instead of telling us to tell them that she don't feel like talking she tell us to tell them she is taking a shower or sleep. What does that teach a child? How to tell a lie. We are taught to doubt ourselves, to be afraid to speak up and speak out because we have been shunned and silenced since childhood. As a child we are not aware of certain things like racism unless we are taught. We were taught that blacks are inferior and whites are superior. Nobody is superior over me but God who has power and all the dominion in both heaven and on Earth. Not a white man, not the president or anybody else for that matter. We are taught about money and materialistic things of this world that is being idolized by man. We are taught that in order to be blessed a miraculous thing has to occur in our lives. Some preachers even preach about money and teach that in order to be given something you must pay your tithes, offerings, first fruit, second offering, peace offering, seed offering, etc.

I'm not saying that if you don't give you won't receive. But what I am saying is that giving has been taken out of context and is used crookedly for personal gain. There is more to giving then just money. You have some preachers who got the gift of proph-a-lying (false prophecy) just to make money, promising people that they will be given a car, house or whatever. People please understand that everybody is not going to be rich, I don't care how save you are. When God speaks about riches He is not talking about the riches in this World but those that are in heaven. We are taught from the internet, television and magazines that in order to feel and be beautiful or handsome is to be skinny or muscle toned on the cover of a magazine. We are taught sexy is to show as much skin as possible. We are taught that it is okay to have sex before marriage as long as you care for that person and use protection. Homosexuality and lesbianism is being accepted to the point that they can get married from one state or country to the next. Do not let the foolishness of this world overcrowd your judgment. Get in the Word, ask God for wisdom and learn something so that you can teach somebody else about something that's worth learning.

Change Your Atmosphere

"Peace, I leave with you, my peace I give unto you: not as the world giveth, I unto you." ~ *John 14: 27*

Change Your Atmosphere

10

"*I* call heaven and earth as witnesses today against you, that I have set before you life and death, blessing and cursing; therefore choose life, that both you and your descendants may live (Deuteronomy 30:19). So, in other words, the choices of the present generations would determine the direction of future generations (NKJV Amplified Bible). But by the grace of God I was brought up out of the curse. I looked at how my uncles, aunts, cousins, etc. lived and made my mind up that the breaking of the curse starts with me. I will not be condemned or stuck in the curse that was cast on my forefathers. The devil will have no reign over me. Change had to come and I had to make a complete change. And I tell you once you change, the people around you may not like it and then claim you think you better just because you made a choice to break the cycle and do something purposeful with your life. Don't worry, them saying that just lets you know that you are doing something right.

I DIDN'T REALIZE how much negative energy I carried with me from my childhood into my adulthood. There are some who didn't grow up in life but was raised up in the curse. My atmosphere was filled with drama, pettiness, strife and stupidity. Every since I can remember, I was always around fighting, cursing, and arguing. I didn't know what it was like to have a "normal" and stable family. Well I can remember the times that my family would try to get along on the holidays. Growing up was not hard for me, thanks to my grandmother she made sure I was well taken care of. But in those times I have seen things that no child should have to see and I had to hear things that could corrupt any child's mind. I saw aunties and uncles high from drugs and always in and out of prison. I saw my grandmother being disrespected and used in more ways than one. I saw family members stealing from her and cursing her out as if she was nothing to them. I saw her tears and the pain she felt from what she had to go through.

I saw her defenseless cause she was in a wheel chair and unable to do anything for herself. I saw a few of my uncles beat on women and I had an uncle that once used the tube from my grandmother's oxygen concentrator to beat me with. I never forgot that day because the scars that were left burned like crazy. I sat down in front of a fan, hoping that the cool breeze from it will quench the burning from my welts. I saw my aunties fighting like they were fighting a stranger in the streets. They all hate to admit that they are jealous of one another and when they do come together it's always some drama by the end of the day. In my family you can't win for losing. If you do something wrong they talk about you and if you do something right you think you better than the next. I grew up around people who had no motivation, who didn't teach the young about the ups and downs of life. I had to learn from their bad choices and the consequences that resulted from their careless mistakes. I grew up before I could appreciate the qualities of being a child. When my grandmother needed someone to stay with her because her kids didn't have time, I had to stay out of school so she wouldn't be alone.

By the age of eight, I was cooking, cleaning out cluttered closets, scrubbing the toilet, mopping floors, washing clothes and everything else. Some of you have atmospheres that are not attractive. Sad to say, I brought some of those same components learned in my childhood atmosphere to my adulthood. There have been times where I've taken without asking, cursed without feeling embarrassed, caused pain without the hint of remorse because as long as I wasn't getting hurt in the process then it didn't matter, worrying over things that I couldn't change and stressed out about a life that I created on my own. There was at least one good thing that I learned from my childhood and that was having the ability to clean a house. I can't stand a nasty house but deep in my internal house, which is my body, was filthy.

My attic held so many past memories that I stored in boxes leaving it to clutter my space; stuff that I carried from my childhood that I refused to throw away and the broken stuff from my upbringing. In my bedroom where my most intimate moments occurred, was overcrowded with room from my own insecurities about love, desire and my partner. My bathroom was filled with problems that I stored from lack of self-esteem because of my weight gain and the feelings of never feeling quite pretty enough. In my kitchen I wasn't being fed properly. I was malnourished, lacking spiritual food. There were some missing ingredients that were missing in my recipe. In my family room I was so close to those who loved me but yet so far. In my office I stressed over unpaid bills, my inability to find a job and the aggravation of not having enough; the stress of having poor credit report and a bad background record. The rooms in my house were filled with chaos.

I didn't even have happiness or peace within my own home. Then I had to question myself. Do I have some folks in the wrong room? Who has the keys to my house? Who is it that has access to my emotional house that is causing me to not have peace in my own home? Who have I collected my spare keys from, and why haven't I changed the old locks? Do I completely trust those who I have entrusted with the keys to my house currently? If I lose the key to my emotional wholeness, who can I rely on to get me back in? Who knows where my keys are hidden? Who am I letting in my house, in my world and in my atmosphere? There are patterns that I have that are still hard to break and there were patterns that I had that the devil used against me. He knew what buttons to push and what emotions to stir up to get a reaction out of me.

That's how the devil operates. He knows who to bring into our space to shake us up and cause total chaos in our lives. There are some things that the devil can bring up and use against me that don't even matter now. That's because I don't give him the satisfaction of thinking that what he do matters to me. You know when you have come to a level of spiritual maturity when your response to what the devil throws at you changes.

The funny thing is, I have been around a few saved folks who have no peace at all. These are the saved folks that attended church every Sunday, run all up and through the church, dance all around the pulpit, clap their hands and do their dance to sound of the beating drum. They can quote scriptures backwards and spend hours in worship on the floor blanketed by the "Holy Spirit" but have absolutely no peace. They reside in a home that's filled with inclusive chaos. Many do not realize this but whatever atmosphere you dwell in you will bring all of that into your house and into your atmosphere. I always wondered why at times my significant other didn't want to spend time with me or my own child hesitated before coming in my room. But I noticed that they didn't do these things because they didn't love me but it was because they didn't want to be in my atmosphere. Have you ever came across someone who is always depressed, never happy with nothing good to say and even when you walk in their home your spirit starts sinking and all of a sudden you being to feel unhappy?

People like that wonder why they are alone, it's because can't nobody stand to be around them let alone live with them. Nobody wants to be around someone with an atmosphere filled with dejection, depression, aggravation, perplexity, negativity and anxiety. There were times when I would be just fine until I go through some financial problems. My peace was in my stuff (material things) and the devil knew just what to do to take away my peace, but when I became wiser and grew up to another level stuff no longer mattered to me. And you know what, I did not get the victory out of getting my stuff back but my victory was established when I resisted the temptation to give up my peace.

Once upon a time the devil had me losing sleep cause I couldn't pay a bill or stressing over trying to find a job, but when I start applying my life to the Word of God and begin to realize that all I needed to do was be still and know that God was God and He could do exceedingly and abundantly above all that I can ask or think, I developed some peace. There are still some areas that God has to work on within me. I may have gotten pass some things but the devil is always trying to figure out what more he can do, but I constantly seek the peace that Jesus gives. Jesus said peace I leave with you my peace not yours, give I unto thee. He doesn't give the type of peace the world gives.

SPIRITUAL PEACE VERSUS WORLDLY PEACE

Spiritual peace is different from worldly peace. Spiritual peace is given to you from the Lord. It is the type of peace that remains even through your tough times. No matter what you're going through and what situation you are facing at that time that spiritual peace is still there. It comforts you and reassures you. Spiritual peace is that crazy kind of peace. People think you have lost your mind when they see you. You have lost your house, your car and all you've worked hard for and when they see you, you smiling and acting like nothing has happened. Worldly peace is being comfortable with the things that are going on in your world and in your atmosphere. It's those materialistic things that you hold on too that secures you. You are okay as long as everything is calm, cool and collected. When there are no threats, problems or over balanced accounts.

You don't have to worry about your bills, your wife or your husband, your kids and other things like that. You don't have to worry about violence in your neighborhood because you live in an upscale gated community and you don't have to worry about a cut off notice because you make more then enough. Knowing that you can pay your bills and is safe is okay, I'm not saying that but it's something that shifts and will not last long and neither will your peace. God did not send His people into this world to be controlled by it. He gives us that peace that surpasses all understanding. T.D. Jakes calls this type of peace mind boggling, crazy and insane. Peace that looks like you don't know what's going on in your life, peace that means that you don't respond to the circumstances or the situation. I would love that kind of peace. I want to dwell in an atmosphere filled with an incredibly insane amount of peace that quenches my thirst because I realize that I cannot do anything practical or beneficial in a chaotic atmosphere.

I want that spiritual peace that the Lord gives. That type of peace that resist the atmosphere of this world so that I can dwell in atmosphere of complete inviolability and peace. At times I can be easily annoyed, easily distracted and agitated, so when I get like that I either shut myself in my room and talk with God or I take a walk and talk to God. People would pass me and look at me like I'm crazy, looking around trying to figure out who I'm talking to. Many times I don't get a response from God but it gives me peace of mind knowing that He is listening. It gives me peace to cast all my problems and cares on Him. I can get all my problems out without being interrupted, misunderstood or misinterpreted. God is not asking you to walk around like a loon because life does not gives us the luxury of walking around like we are out of space, but there is a place you can get in God where nothing else matters. It's a place of secrecy between you and God. I can get behind the veil and He reaches me.

God does not want us to drown in our situations and/or circumstances. You don't have to stress out and let life get to you. I speak peace into your heart and into your life. I understand that we go through life's struggles and that everyday we are battling with the tragedies of this world. I know we have responsibilities that we have to deal with each day but each and every day you need to be given something. Get you some peace. You can't buy it but the Prince of Peace, which is Jesus Christ, can give it you. The devil don't want us to have peace, it is his goal to keep us bottled up in our misery for as long as he can. He knows that as long as your mind is in that peaceful zone, there would be no way of him getting in. God procreate and birth in us fruitful things when we are in a peaceful state.

DO NOT WORRY

I'm saying it just as bold as you see it. DO NOT WORRY! I know most people do just that when they are clueless of how to move or where to go in a situation. When God didn't do what they hoped He would do; when He moved one way and they move another. When the plan they had for their life ends up being nothing like they imagined. When you thought your husband was at work only to call the office and realize that he left two hours ago. When your wife ends up pregnant and you've just got laid off from your job. What do you do? Worry. God does not want us to worry. Just like He takes care of the grass in the field, so will He take care of us: "And why take ye thought for raiment? Consider the lilies of the field, how they grow; they toil not, neither do they spin: And yet I say unto you, that even Solomon in all his glory was not arrayed like one of these. Wherefore, if God so clothe the grass of the field, which today is, and tomorrow is cast into the oven, shall he not much more clothe you, O ye of little faith? Do not worry then, saying, 'What will we eat?' or 'What will we drink?' or 'What will we wear for clothing? For the Gentiles eagerly seek all these things; for your heavenly Father knows that you need all these things. But seek first His kingdom and His righteousness, and all these things will be added to you. So do not worry about tomorrow; for tomorrow will care for itself. Each day has enough trouble of its own (Matthew 6:28-35). When you start seeking God first, everything that you need He will give to you. Stop magnifying the problem and magnify God. Stop dwelling on the same things over and over again and know that God is able. Stop seeking the things of this world and seek God and He will open up the windows of heaven and pour you out a blessing that you want have room enough to receive. Everybody has gone through something but it has not killed them. Even Abraham had to go through some things to get to the blessing in which God had for him. You can't worry about something you can't change. You have got to get you some spiritual peace.

Don't just speak it, live in it. You cannot speak what you don't reside in. Jesus told His disciples that He is going to leave them His peace. That same peace He had when He slept through the storm when they were out in the boat. We all have storms but God has His way of getting us through those storms. He didn't say He was going to stop the storm from coming; He'll just help us with a little peace. The reality is, we are all going to have to deal with things in this world and some things will be here today and gone tomorrow. If you can't afford a house payment, rent an apartment. If you know the parts to a Mercedes is worth more than you are able to afford get yourself a Honda, it'll last longer. The toilet will clog up, bills are sure to come and eventually if you use the hot water too long the water is going to get cold. And another thing, stop living above your means, if you know your spending habits is bigger than your paycheck then budget.

We can avoid some situations from happening. We are going to go through some stuff in this world that we do not want to go through but we cannot allow it to take away our peace. We have to be able to let the world operate and let life run its course without worrying about the affects of change. Trade in your peace for God's in watch how your whole atmosphere changes.

Being Different is Beautiful

"No one has the exact same mix of factors that make you unique. That means no one else on earth will ever be able to play the role God planned for you." ~ Rick Warren

The Beauty of Being Different

11

LET ME TELL YOU something, being different is beautiful. It's an amazing thing knowing that you don't have the same qualities as other folks. It does not make a difference what skin you're in, where you come from or what side of the tracks you were brought up in, we all are important and have meaning. So, what her hair is longer than yours, they have many beauty supply stores that can sale you some and guess what, you can choose any length you want. Better yet, take better care of your hair, get helpful tips how to get your hair to its healthiest potential that way it will grow. You got black eyes but want some hazel ones, go get you some contacts they have them in a variety of colors. You can be hazel one day and blue eyed the next, it's your world. If God wanted you to have a different color eyes He would have given it to you. If you want to be skinny, diet and exercise. You don't have to stay overweight; you have a choice and the right to shed some pounds. However, don't do it for someone else, do it for yourself. Do it because it is something that will make you feel better. You can't try to meet everyone's expectations and if they can't accept the way you look then leave them be.

My great mistake, the fault for which I can't forgive myself is that one day I ceased my obstinate pursuit of my own individuality.

~Oscar Wilde

Too many people are so worried about what people think about them that they can't even be themselves. You're not going to be able to be friends with everyone. And there are some people who may not like you and that's okay. You have enemies? Good. That only means that at some point in your life you've stood up for something. Be yourself. Love who you are. Young lady, you don't have to look like anybody else to be beautiful. You don't have to have a body like any of these models or celebrities to feel vibrant and you do not have to expose your body to get attention. Your beauty speaks for itself. If he can't accept who you are in the inside then he want respect your outer appearance either. If he isn't looking in your eyes, but at your chest and your behind then you already know he don't care about your mind. You won't get respect unless you demand it and respect won't be given unless you stand firm to what you believe in. Don't let a guy pursue you into doing something you are not ready to do, if he care enough about you then he'll wait and if he can wait then he's letting you know that you're worth it.

Don't fall for, "oh if you give it up, my feelings for you won't change, or if you have sex with me it will show how much you really love me." Stand up for yourself and when you do, you'll feel good knowing that you made the right decision. Young man, learn to be a leader not a follower. If you know that your friends are doing something wrong, don't follow let them know that it is wrong. Because real friends won't do anything or tell you to do anything wrong. Stay in school, get that education and be somebody in life. You have a choice to choose how your life will end up. Do not be another statistic; make a difference for yourself and other young men to come. If you got a little brother, make better decisions for him, if you have a son be a better example for him and tell him the mistakes you made and how you made a change.

There are some women who have husbands that cheat on them because he said that they were too fat, so they spend countless of hours trying to shed the weight and some will not even eat just to get the weight off and when they get the weight off, he still cheating. You will even be bold enough to ask him, "What does she do for you that I can't? I can be that woman you want me to be? I can be her." If the other woman got blond hair, you will go dye your hair blond or get a blond wig. If she wears red lip stick you will go get you some. Some woman will go to the moon and back just to keep that man from cheating. You can do all you can to keep him from cheating, but if he wants to cheat he's going to. I don't care if you cut your hair like Halle Berry and go get some plastic surgery and make a few changes, he still going to do what he wants to do. It doesn't have anything to do with you; it has everything to do with him.

You can't spend your whole life centered around another, you'll forget yourself. You want to change, that's fantastic, develop some advantageous ways of changing. Become the change that you wish to see in the world. Embrace the changes you have made in your life, especially if they are positive changes. I've had to change who I associate with and I am very careful as to who I allow in my corner. Not because I think that I am better but because I have to be careful as to whom I allow in my world and in my atmosphere. There is no place I'd rather be then to be in the presence of the Lord and there is no other way I'd rather be then to be who God has created me to be. Being right with God makes you different. I love serving God and I love living according to His ways. Beware my fellow God seekers. Be aware that being different has always had its disadvantages.

Jesus was whipped, mocked and persecuted for being who He was. He changed the Israelites whole way of believing. He was only doing what he was destined to do. He had His own uniqueness that any of them failed to have and that infuriated them. His own disciples turned away from Him, one deceived Him and one disowned Him. There are people who you thought that would love you forever who will turn their backs on you because of your transformation. Don't fret when your so-called friends turn their back on you because of that change. Don't feel disappointed when the "love of your life" wants to break it off with you because of your change. They will say that you've altered into someone that they don't know anymore. Your choices are not the same, the words you use are different and your reaction to situations is not how they use to be. You aren't the same person in which you use to be, you have changed.

You have reached a level of maturity that is far above that in which you use to have, therefore, if you have friends and/or associates that is still on the level in which you once was they are incompetent of who you are now; because when God changes you into the person that your are purposed to be, that "different you", they are blinded and has no comprehension of the new you. When you are no longer living to worldly standards and to other people's standards, you will get a different reaction out of people. Your current values do not match up with others and those who feel threatened by you will react in fury and malevolence. That integrity and moral strength you have obtained intimidates those who lacks inner strength and they may choose to turn on you. "If ye were of the world, the world would love his own; but because ye are not of this world, but I have chosen you out of the world, therefore the world hateth you (John 15:19)."

When this happens to you in life, God wants you to still be happy. God loves those who love Him and delights in those who are willing to stand up for His Word. Just like Jesus, you are only doing what you are destined to do and being who you are destined to be. Something outstanding is in a person when they can stand to be humiliated and still have peace through their humiliation. At some point in our lives we will all have to face humiliation, persecution, and being ridiculed and mocked, but through it all we still have Jesus, who is our strength. Yes, Jesus suffered a great deal but He got the victory in the end. So hold your head up high lift it up to the hills and walk in your uniqueness, walk in your change and walk in your beauty. Because just like Jesus had to suffer to get His crown, so will you to reap eternal life. "Blessed are they which are persecuted for righteousness' sake; for theirs is the kingdom of heaven (Matthew 5:10)."

I do not need anyone's permission, consent or approval to be who I am, my true self. I don't accept stereotypes and I have no need to conform to the stereotypes others have defined for me. I've never had a problem when people dismiss themselves out of my life and I've never had a problem with dismissing others out of mine. I just don't get too close to people like that to care. Maybe that sounds harsh, I wouldn't know, you decide, but if I cared about each and every person that wanted to leave me then I'll be messed up. I've had people in my life that I truly cared for that I called a friend that ended up talking behind my back. I've had men in my life that didn't always come through with their end of the bargain. I've got family members who are much worst than an enemy. But guess what, I don't live for the people of this world, I live for God.

When we allow ourselves to exist truly and fully, we sting the world with our vision and challenge it with our own ways of being.
~Thomas Moore

People will come and go out of your life, but you have to know when a person season is up. Don't mix seasonal people with life time expectations, when they are ready to go, let them go. When they want to act out of character, let them play on stage by themselves, they can create their own audience. Always be yourself, don't deny who you are to appease to anyone. Embrace change, embrace wanting to be different and to being better than who you once where, there isn't any shame in that. People will not only know that you have changed because of your actions and attitude but they will know that you've changed because of the way you look. When people look at you they will see blessed. When God changes you, it's a certain glow He sets on you that can be seen a mile away. When Jesus stepped into every city to preach, they recognized Him, they follow Him and they wanted to be close to Him.

There are some folks who will draw near to you just because of what God has laid upon you, but be careful because some folks will come to suck away all your beauty. Serving God and getting a complete makeover is a beautiful thing. Everyone is not going to understand or support your beliefs. No worries, just give it all over to God and He'll do the rest. You are not made to please everyone, but to be pleasing unto God. Don't hold on to the old stuff when God is trying to make you into the woman or man He want you to be. If your friends can't respect that you have given your life to God, then guess what, it's time to change who you associate with. God has His way of shifting people out of your life that does not coincide with your level of change. When we have made up in our minds to live for God, most likely He will do some renovation in you and in your environment. You may not have that same boyfriend or girlfriend no more, so what, God is going to prepare you for your husband or wife to come. Your best buddy may become your worst enemy and your own family may come against you but that's okay because God can send you a spiritual family that will be your support system and if all that isn't enough just know if you don't have anyone else you got Jesus.

My Adam-His Eve... My Boaz-His Ruth
The Seriousness of Love & Marriage

A great marriage is not when the 'perfect couple' come together.
It is   when an imperfect couple learns to enjoy their differences.
~Dave Meurer

My Adam-His Eve... My Boaz-His Ruth The Seriousness of Love & Marriage

12

NOW I KNOW you're wondering, what does marriage have to do with me discovering who I am? My answer to that is... nothing. However, marriage plays a major part of what you will become in your role as a spouse. The one who you decide to spend the rest of your life with, will become apart of you, making you both one. There is something divine, sacred and magical about the creation of Eve. God knew that it was not good for Adam to be alone, so He decided to make a helper *suitable* for him. God didn't say He asked Adam to help Him select and design the person of his choice. No. God gave Adam what He needed which goes beyond all the things he could have wanted.

Suitable.

This means He made someone similar to Adam. Appropriate. Obsolete. Adam didn't know what God was doing or how He did it because according to "the good book", God put Adam in a deep sleep and as he was sleeping, He took one rib from Adam and closed up the wound. Then God made a woman from the rib that He had taken from Adam and *brought* her to the man. Then Adam said, "This is now bone of my bones and flesh of my flesh". God's use of a rib was fitting. Do you understand the sacredness of what Adam said? *Bone of my bones and flesh of my flesh*. The match was perfect and she was a reflection of him, yet different. This means there is no subordination between a female and a male but only partnership, respect, unity and sharing. It is not about one being dominant over the other but sharing their dominance between one another. There is something when you've married someone who you think is for you but there is something else when you've married someone who God has *brought* to you. God made Eve for Adam from his rib, fitting and perfect.

Don't mistake it...just because God made Adam for Eve doesn't mean that the one you with was made for you. And just because Henry told you that you two are meant for each other does not mean that you are. If God told him that He can tell you too. God does things in decent and in order and He also sends confirmation behind everything He say. So if He showed him, He will show you too. Every rib that comes your way is not going to fit. Look at your mate and think about it, dissect and get your X-ray out. Are your ribs matching? Many times people find themselves in bad relationships and enduring messy divorces because they are too busy doing the fishing with unhealthy bate. Why go out and catch a cat fish when God can bring you some Arowana? Even the story of how Ruth and Boaz met was beautiful and significant. They did not meet by chance, but there was something supernatural that joined them together. It takes time to find your Adam and your Eve and a love like Ruth and Boaz.

In marriage, each partner is to be an encourager rather than a critic, a forgiver rather than a collector of hurts, an enabler rather than a reformer. ~*H. Norman Wright and Gary J. Oliver*

When I see an old couple who has been together for 30 and 50 years and still have that fire in their heart for one another I smile and I hope that when my time comes that I'd still be able to find who my heart loves and be able to still look him in the eyes 30 years from now and still be able to say "I love you and I still want you." You have to first be friends before becoming a couple and actually be a couple before jumping the broom. Marriage is not like it used to be; in those times when commitment was golden. When you not only marry your man but you marry your best friend. When I ask an old couple what keeps them holding on to each other, I always get the same answer, love. You have to be able to have enough love in you that it's able to withstand any hardship that comes your way. You have to be able go through some ups and downs and understand that a relationship is not all about waterfalls and rainbows. You have to be able to communicate effectively and truly understand where each other is coming from. To compromise, to look beyond self, beyond one's faults and still be able to say, "You're still the one".

Now, here's what people don't understand about some long marriages. Some long marriages withstand infidelity, financial difficulties, hardships and even abuse. You have some who stay for the kids and once the kids grow up they figure that they might as well stay. You have some who stay for the stability and because they do not won't to start over. There are many reasons why a person stays in a marriage; all reasons are not the same. But the point I'm trying to make is marriage is all about being able to endure the good days and the rainy days, it's about having enough respect for one another. It's about trust, patience, faith, and sincerity. We all dream of having a fairy tale ending with our love, but the reality is relationships are not to be built on fairytales. You're never going to get that kind of love that you see in fairytales and on the movies but if you get something close to it, then you're blessed.

You can live to say that you have had the blessings of being with your true Adam/Eve. When you're able to know for a fact that the man or woman you with is the one that you want to spend the rest of your life with you have accomplished something that many have failed at accomplishing. Often times people jump into relationships without knowing the history of the one they are with. They don't know where they come from, who they came from, and what they carry with them from their past. Their past hurts, generational toxins that they learned from childhood, and what they're "really" about. It's important to know who you are dating before you decide to marry them. What tragedy are they holding on to from their past? Are they married? Are they *really* divorced? Have they really gotten over there past relationships? What makes them tick? What calms them? What kind of job do they work at? Do they like kids? Do they have kids? Do they have excellent, good, fair or bad credit? Do they have a background record, if so what's on it? Do they love God?

It is important to know how they present themselves to you. If they aren't showing you who they are wait a little while longer because eventually their true colors will come out. Pay attention to the signs, the patterns and what they are truly saying when they are talking to you. There are some who don't even know their mates favorite color, favorite food or whether they like their eggs scrambled or fried. Then women want to get mad when that man end up being a pedophile or living a double life. Or the man gets mad when the woman ends up being with him only for his money. Some people say, well they didn't show me that until after we got married or years later into the relationship, but had you really been paying attention you would know the signs were already there. You get so involved with your heart that you lose all your common sense. Some say love can do that to you. No, we have already established that love doesn't hurt anyone. What do it to you is when you make hasty decisions based on your own feelings and your poor listening skills when you've prayed about it.

That's what happens when you move too fast. It takes time to know someone and even longer to build a solid foundation that can withstand all the challenges that comes in a marriage. For a while it will be as if you're still on your honeymoon but after time passes by and the infatuation fades, something else has to be able to keep that fire burning. We live in a time where everything is done in an instant. Where chapters of a book are only half completed and the full story is left unread. We'd rather rush to get to the ending of the story without getting the insight of how the story got its ending. We have everything from instant sermons to instant prayer from instant relationships to instant marriages. Some never sit and patiently think things through these days. For instance, you can't expect instant potatoes to taste like homemade potatoes. In instant potatoes all you have to do is add a little water or milk but when you have homemade potatoes you boil natural potatoes. You wait until they boil to perfection, then you add your milk, butter, mayo (if you prefer), a little salt and pepper.

You may want to add some sour cream and chives to it. See good things take more work and more time. Patience is a virtue. You have to know the value of patience. In everything God made, He took His time creating it. He did not rush to make heaven, Earth nor man. It took Him days to create the things we see today. He could have made it all in an instant, but He knew the significance of doing things with patience. See, when we quickly do things we tend to leave out small but important details and find ourselves having to go back and do it all over again. There is nothing wrong with patiently waiting; in fact you'll later find that waiting for what you want is always worth it in the end. I've been around many single people who say, "God is going to send me a husband", that could very well be true, but it takes time for that as well.

God can be preparing that mate for you and it may seem like years before he/she come but it is only because the man or woman you may be meant to be with could still be going through what they are going through in order to get the experience, knowledge and wisdom that they need to have in order to be prepared for you. But you cannot expect your Boaz to come to you when you got Herbert, Michael or Tom living there with you. Understand that the husband or wife you've being praying to God for cannot come into a space that is already rented out. You want a husband but you're holding on to too many things. You got to many toothbrushes in your toothbrush holder in your personal bathroom. You have too many clothes and shoes that are not yours in your closet. Get rid of the access baggage so that your new wardrobe can be delivered. Let's talk about the list. Now we all got a list of qualities a man or woman must have before you want to marry them.

I admit that I did have a list of what I wanted my husband to be like. I just had to have a man that did not have kids (but loved kids), who was content, stable, handsome, romantic, intelligent, adventurous, dependent enough to let me take control, but independent enough to control what needed to be controlled, and someone who have no desire to be with a man, another woman, or a child (hey you never know). But I realized that often times people can have unrealistic standards. I am not telling anyone to lower their standards, but I am saying that you may have to make some adjustments and accept that there is no such thing as "perfect." Even still, there is some things on my list I cannot do without. For instance: I have to have someone in my life who loves the Lord. Someone who can read the Bible with me, pray with me, fellowship with me, and speak life into me when I feel like throwing in the towel. Someone who driven, purposed, reliable, trusting, faithful, caring and loving. Not too bad, right? There are some who may want their wife to be smart, sexy, independent or dependent (depending on the man) and wholesome. A woman may want her husband to be successful, good looking, prestigious and all those beautiful qualities. But what we often fail to think about is whether that man or woman on our list would want to be with us. You may just come across a man or a woman with most or all of those qualities but will that other person's list match you? Will you be the woman/man that he/ she is looking for?

We all have flaws but we try to search for someone perfect instead of acknowledging that nobody is perfect. You have to find someone who is perfect for you, while accepting their flaws in the same token. We would never be able to find the perfect mate because we are all imperfect, if we were all able to accept the imperfectness of each other then we may be able to hold a relationship for a little while longer. There is no such thing as a perfect relationship and you cannot make someone be someone that they are not. You have to both treat each other like you want to be treated. And women stop thinking that you're always right because you're not. You are capable of being wrong some of the time. Learn to let that man be a man and men respect that woman like you would want a man to respect your daughter or your mother. Don't just say "I love you" to anyone be sure that, that person is someone that you really love and not someone you lust. When you love, love for real.

Don't just tell someone what they want to hear. Marriage is not going to save the relationship nor is having a child by that man is going to make him marry you. If she or he is doing wrong while you are dating rest assured it's not going to change when you say, "I do." Marriage shouldn't be about convenience but about a sacred love that is joined together by God. It's not okay to jump from marriage to marriage and it should not be that easy for couples to get a divorce. Couples are not willing to fight like they use to. They don't want to take the effort and do what it takes to make it work. It is so easy to just leave or just jump in the bed with another. That's not what God intended for marriage to be. So make sure you understand the seriousness of marriage and everything it brings before you get married. You have to know beyond a shadow of a doubt that the person you're with is who you want to be with for the rest of your life. Take a moment and close your eyes and when you close your eyes imagine the person you would like to be your husband or wife. Do you see yourself having kids with them?

Do you see yourself old in age holding hands, rocking in a rocking chair on your porch? Is it the one who is lying beside you? Is it that same person that you call your boo? Some may say, "Yeah, at that moment I did see it but as the years went by what I once saw was not there anymore." That's because you were seeing with your mind and not with your heart. It is possible to *think* that a person is for you and as you begin to meditate on those thoughts, you begin to *feel* that the person is for you. Many mistake these feelings as heartfelt feelings when they are only feelings that you have thought up. Your mind and your heart must come together in agreement and if one doesn't agree with the other than you need to wait a little while longer. If you're not ready then don't do it but if you are ready be prepared for the task at hand then by all means jump that broom. And men please stop trying to throw the scripture at us about a woman's role. You're skipping some of it.

Often men take the Bible out of context when it comes to a woman's role as a wife. Yes, it does say, "Wives submit to your *own* (not someone else's) husbands, as to the Lord. For the husband is head of the wife, as also Christ is head of the church; and He is the Savior of the body. Therefore just as the church is subject to Christ so let the wives be to their own husbands in everything (Ephesians 5:22-24)." This verse does not mean that a woman is inferior to a man nor is Christ inferior to God, but Jesus is apart of God, made One. Just like a husband in his wife is made as one when they get married, which makes them both equal to one another. Furthermore, "Husbands ought to love their wives, just as Christ also loved the church and gave Himself for her, that He might present her to Himself a glorious church. So husbands ought to love their own (not someone else's) wives as their own bodies he who love his wife loves himself; for no one ever hated his own flesh, but nourishes and cherishes it (Ephesians 6: 25-29)."

Men you have to realize that your wife is not your slave or your punching bag, she is your helpmate, your friend and most importantly she is your own flesh. I'm sure that you don't mentally, physically and/or emotionally abuse yourself, so why do her like that? When you do that to her you are not only hurting her but yourself as well but not only that you're sending negative messages to the Lord. When you find yourself a wife you find yourself a good thing, so don't treat her like your enemy, treat her like the jewel she is. To find a wife is another thing but to find a virtuous woman is another, she is worth more than rubies. She does what is supposed to be done without hesitation. Women wait for your Adam or your Boaz. Men make sure you've found your Eve or your Ruth. Once Adam is connected to Eve and Ruth has found her Boaz then marriage is worth the sacrifice and the work that has to be put in it. Know who you are marrying, be patient and wait. Anything worth having is definitely worth waiting for. You should not have to regret being married but appreciate the beauty of being married and finding that someone who is willing to marry you.

Words of Encouragement

When you feel like giving up, just remind yourself of what you have endured already and remember why you held on for so long in the first place. ~ Kezia Davis

Words of Encouragement

THERE IS NOTHING I love more than to open a book that can encourage me for the day. There are some people that do not understand the Bible or may not know where to go in the Word to receive comfort. This chapter is for those who are incarcerated and for those who has no idea of what to look for in the Bible. In this chapter I will just include a list of encouraging psalms and Bible verses that will help motivate you and inspire you when you need it. Often times we just need words of encouragement to lift us up and I hope I can provide you with some that will uplift your spirit in the Lord. As I was writing this book, I realized how much I was motivating myself. All the helpful sources (T.D. Jakes, Iyanla Vanzant, etc.) that I used in this book have been my encouragers when I need to be encouraged. There words speak volumes and they may not know each and every life that they touch, but I'm sending my blessings to them through this book and through my prayers. God bless you all and I pray that this book can be as helpful to you as it's been for me.

BIBLE VERSUS & PSALMS

- The LORD is my shepherd; I shall not want. He maketh me to lie down in green pastures: he leadeth me beside the still waters. He restoreth my soul: he leadeth me in the paths of righteousness for his name's sake. Yea, though I walk through the valley of the shadow of death, I will fear no evil: for thou art with me; thy rod and thy staff they comfort me. Thou preparest a table before me in the presence of mine enemies: thou anointest my head with oil; my cup runneth over. Surely goodness and mercy shall follow me all the days of my life: and I will dwell in the house of the LORD for ever *(Psalm 23)*.
- Rise up; this matter is in your hands. We will support you, so take courage and do it *(Ezra 10:4)*.
- But even if you should suffer for what is right, you are blessed. Do not fear what they fear; do not be frightened *(1 Peter 3:14)*.
- So do not fear, for I am with you; do not be dismayed, for I am your God. I will strengthen you and help you; I will uphold you with my righteous

right hand *(Isaiah 41:10).*

- LORD, you have assigned me my portion and my cup; you have made my lot secure. The boundary lines have fallen for me in pleasant places; surely I have a delightful inheritance. I will praise the LORD, who counsels me; even at night my heart instructs me. I have set the LORD always before me. Because he is at my right hand, I will not be shaken *(Psalm 16:5-8).*

- It is God who arms me with strength and makes my way perfect. He makes my feet like the feet of a deer; he enables me to stand on the heights. He trains my hands for battle; my arms can bend a bow of bronze. You give me your shield of victory, and your right hand sustains me; you stoop down to make me great. You broaden the path beneath me, so that my ankles do not turn *(Psalm 18: 32-36).*

- Show me your ways, O LORD, teach me your paths; guide me in your truth and teach me, for you are God my Savior, and my hope is in you all day long. Remember, O LORD, your great mercy and love, for they are from of old. Remember not the sins of my youth and my rebellious ways; according to your love remember me, for you are good, O LORD *(Psalm 25:4-7).*

- The LORD is my strength and my shield; my heart trusts in him, and I am helped. My heart leaps for joy and I will give thanks to him in song. The LORD is the strength of his people, a fortress of salvation for his anointed one. Save your people and bless your inheritance; be their shepherd and carry them forever *(Psalm 28:7-9).*

- The LORD is my rock, my fortress and my deliverer; my God is my rock, in whom I take refuge. He is my shield and the horn of my salvation, my stronghold. I call to the LORD, who is worthy of praise, and I am saved from my enemies. The cords of death entangled me; the torrents of destruction overwhelmed me. The cords of the grave coiled around me; the snares of death confronted me. In my distress I called to the LORD; I cried to my God for help. From his temple he heard my voice; my cry came before him, into his ears *(Psalms 18:2-6).*

- Commit to the LORD whatever you do, and your plans will succeed *(Proverbs 16:3).*

- *Trust in the LORD, and do good; so shalt thou dwell in the land, and verily thou shalt be fed. Delight thyself also in the LORD; and he shall give thee the desires of thine heart. Commit thy way unto the LORD; trust also in him; and he shall bring it to pass. And he shall bring forth thy righteousness as the light, and thy judgment as the noonday. Rest in the LORD, and wait patiently for him: fret not thyself because of him who prospereth in his way, because of the man who bringeth wicked devices to pass. Cease from anger, and forsake wrath: fret not thyself in any wise to do evil. For evildoers shall be cut off: but those that wait upon the LORD, they shall inherit the earth. For yet a little while, and the wicked shall not be: yea, thou shalt diligently consider his place, and it shall not be. But the meek shall inherit the earth; and shall delight themselves in the abundance of peace (Psalms 37:3-11).*

- Blessed are the pure in heart: for they shall see God *(Matthew 5:8).*
- Blessed are the peacemakers: for they shall be called the children of God *(Matthew 5:9).*
- Fight the good fight of the faith. Take hold of the eternal life to which you were called *(1 Timothy 6:12).*
- The name of the Lord is a strong tower; the righteous run to it and are safe *(Proverbs 18:10).*
  Being confident of this, that he who began a good work in you will carry it on to completion until the day of Christ Jesus *(Philippians 1:6).*
- So do not fear, for I am with you; do not be dismayed, for I am your God. I will strengthen you and help you; I will uphold you with my righteous right hand *(Isaiah 41:10).*
- Commit to the Lord whatever you do, and your plans will succeed *(Proverbs 16:3).*
- Yet the Lord longs to be gracious to you; He arises to show you compassion. For the Lord is a God of justice blessed are all who wait for Him *(Isaiah 30:18).*
- For I know the plans I have for you, declares the Lord, plans to prosper you and not to harm you, plans to give you hope and a future *(Jeremiah 29:11).*
- And let us consider how we may spur one another on toward love and good deeds *(Hebrews 10:24).*
- The Lord is good to those whose hope is in Him, to the one who seeks Him *(Lamentations 3:25).*
- Then Christ will make his home in your hearts as you trust in him. Your roots will grow down into God's love and keep you strong. And may you have the power to understand, as all God's people should, how wide, how

long, how high, and how deep his love is. May you experience the love of Christ, though it is too great to understand fully. Then you will be made complete with all the fullness of life and power that comes from God *(Ephesians 3:17-19)*.

- Now all glory to God, who is able, through his mighty power at work within us, to accomplish infinitely more than we might ask or think. Glory to him in the church and in Christ Jesus through all generations forever and ever! Amen *(Ephesians 3:20-21)*.

- And so, dear brothers and sisters, we can boldly enter heaven's Most Holy Place because of the blood of Jesus. By his death, Jesus opened a new and life-giving way through the curtain into the Most Holy Place. And since we have a great High Priest who rules over God's house, let us go right into the presence of God with sincere hearts fully trusting him. For our guilty consciences have been sprinkled with Christ's blood to make us clean, and our bodies have been washed with pure water. Let us hold tightly without wavering to the hope we affirm, for God can be trusted to keep his promise *(Hebrews 10:19-23)*.

- The Sovereign Lord is my strength; He makes my feet like the feet of a deer, He enables me to go on the heights *(Habakkuk 3:19)*.

- Consider it all joy, my brethren, when you encounter various trials, knowing that the testing of your faith produces endurance. And let endurance have its perfect result, so that you may be perfect and complete, lacking in nothing *(James 1:2-4)*.

PRAYER BIBLE VERSUS

- Be still and know that I am God *(Psalm 46:10)*.

- But when you pray, go into your room, close the door and pray to your Father, who is unseen. Then your Father, who sees what is done in secret, will reward you *(Matthew 6:6)*.

- Ask and it will be given to you; seek and you will find; knock and the door will be opened to you. 8For everyone who asks receives; he who seeks finds; and to him who knocks, the door will be opened. 9"Which of you, if his son asks for bread, will give him a stone? 10Or if he asks for a fish, will give him a snake? 11If you, then, though you are evil, know how to give good gifts to your children, how much more will your Father in heaven give good gifts to those who ask him *(Matthew 7:7-11).*

- Again, I tell you that if two of you on earth agree about anything you ask for, it will be done for you by my Father in heaven. For where two or three come together in my name, there am I with them *(Matthew 18:19-20).*
- If you believe, you will receive whatever you ask for in prayer *(Matthew 21:22).*
- Jesus looked at them and said, "With man this is impossible, but not with God; all things are possible with God *(Mark 10:27).*
- Therefore I tell you, whatever you ask for in prayer, believe that you have received it, and it will be yours *(Mark 11:24).*
- On reaching the place, he said to them, "Pray that you will not fall into temptation *(Luke 22:40).*
- So I say to you: Ask and it will be given to you; seek and you will find; knock and the door will be opened to you. 10For everyone who asks receives; he who seeks finds; and to him who knocks, the door will be opened *(Luke 11:9-10).*
- And I will do whatever you ask in my name, so that the Son may bring glory to the Father *(John 14:13).*
- If you remain in me and my words remain in you, ask whatever you wish, and it will be given you *(John 15:7).*
- In that day you will no longer ask me anything. I tell you the truth, my Father will give you whatever you ask in my name *(John 16:23).*
- Now to him who is able to do immeasurably more than all we ask or imagine, according to his power that is at work within us, to him be glory in the church and in Christ Jesus throughout all generations, for ever and ever! Amen *(Ephesians 3:20-21).*
- Let us then approach the throne of grace with confidence, so that we may receive mercy and find grace to help us in our time of need *(Hebrews 4:16).*
- If any of you lacks wisdom, he should ask God, who gives generously to all without finding fault, and it will be given to him. But when he asks, he must believe and not doubt, because he who doubts is like a wave of the sea, blown and tossed by the wind *(James 1:5-6).*
- Therefore confess your sins to each other and pray for each other so that you may be healed. The prayer of a righteous man is powerful and effective *(James 5:16).*
- Dear friends, if our hearts do not condemn us, we have confidence before God

and receive from him anything we ask, because we obey his commands and do what pleases him *(1 John 3:21-22)*.

- This is the confidence we have in approaching God: that if we ask anything according to his will, he hears us. And if we know that he hears us—whatever we ask—we know that we have what we asked of him *(1 John 5:14-15)*.
- Have mercy on me, O God, according to your unfailing love; according to your great compassion blot out my transgressions. Wash away all my iniquity and cleanse me from my sin. For I know my transgressions, and my sin is always before me. Against you, you only, have I sinned and done what is evil in your sight; so you are right in your verdict and justified when you judge. Surely I was sinful at birth, sinful from the time my mother conceived me. Yet you desired faithfulness even in the womb; you taught me wisdom in that secret place. Cleanse me with hyssop, and I will be clean; wash me, and I will be whiter than snow. Let me hear joy and gladness; let the bones you have crushed rejoice. Hide your face from my sins and blot out all my iniquity. Create in me a pure heart, O God, and renew a steadfast spirit within me. Do not cast me from your presence or take your Holy Spirit from me. Restore to me the joy of your salvation and grant me a willing spirit, to sustain me. Then I will teach transgressors your ways, so that sinners will turn back to you. Deliver me from the guilt of bloodshed, O God, you who are God my Savior, and my tongue will sing of your righteousness. Open my lips, Lord, and my mouth will declare your praise. You do not delight in sacrifice, or I would bring it; you do not take pleasure in burnt offerings. My sacrifice, O God, is a broken spirit; a broken and contrite heart you, God, will not despise *(Psalm 51: 1-17)*.

Resources

Whats-Your-Sign.com. (2011). Lily Meaning and Symbolism. From the website, http://www.whats-your-sign.com/lily-meaning 24.html

Beverly Flanigan. (1994). Forgiving the Unforgivable: Overcoming the Legacy of Intimate Wounds. Wiley Publishing.

Input "Rev. Dr. Douglas K. Showalter (1997). Eight Forgiveness Questions To Ponder. From the website, http://www. dougshow.my.cape.com/webdoc2. htm

The Amplified Holy Bible

Iyanla Vanzant.(1996). The Value in The Valley: Black Woman's Guide Through Life's Dilemma. Fireside Publishing.

Sermons: T.D. Jakes (Free Your Mind & Let It Go)

Poem: Chosen One by Heather Will

Dictionary: Knowledge & Wisdom

Thesaurus: Understanding

Peter Sinclair. (n.d.). How To Grow In Wisdom. From the website, http:// www.motivationalmemo.com/how-to-grow-in-wisdom/

You're Invited...

I personally invite you to join my group on Facebook:

Christian's Mingle

As a member you will be entitled to:

- Share your thoughts with fellow Christian's
- Give your advice to others or simply post your thoughts on the wall.
- Meet new people who have the desire to want to know more and help encourage people in God.

Christian's Mingle

www.facebook.com/groups/christiansmingle

Visit my website (www.keziadavis.com) for all the latest updates.

Follow me on:
Facebook
(www.facebook.com/authorkeziadavis)

Twitter
(www.twitter.com/kezia87)

I would love some feedback on what you think of my work. Please feel free to leave your review on whatever site you purchased my work!